UNPRECEDENTED

Teaching in a Pandemic

by Emily Schwickerath

DORRANCE
PUBLISHING CO
EST. 1920
PITTSBURGH, PENNSYLVANIA 15238

Dorrance Publishing Co
585 Alpha Drive
Pittsburgh, PA 15238
Visit our website at *www.dorrancebookstore.com*

ISBN: 978-1-6393-7285-0
eISBN: 978-1-6393-7679-7

UNPRECEDENTED

Teaching in a Pandemic

Contents

For my husband Eric, who has been my solid rock.

For Karen, who helped me get my joy back.

And for all the administrators, teachers, and support staff across the globe who survived this pandemic and didn't give up when things felt impossible.

Acknowledgement

This memoir is written as an ode to the teachers, administrators, support staff, and parents who overcame the unprecedented wave of challenges that Covid-19 presented in 2020 and 2021. I want to recognize that each person, in their unique roles, carries their own experience with the pandemic and that no two people are the same.

My primary reason for writing this book was really as a means of reflection and preservation; recognizing that I am now standing on the other side of a bridge that once seemed impossible to cross. I know that I am not alone in my journey, and my hope is that by sharing my story that others can relate, understand, or gain new perspectives about what the impact of remote learning and hybrid learning has been for teachers.

This is just one story; one experience. For those of you who felt hopeless like I did, who were ready to give up: You are *not* alone.

March 2020
The Month the World Stopped

MADNESS, PURE CHAOS.

My husband, Eric, and I always used to joke about how unfair it was that he had the ability to work from home. You see, he works in marketing and in 2019, his company decided that they would allow all their employees to choose one day to work in a remote setting. I would smile as I walk out the door on Friday mornings, thinking, *"Wouldn't it be nice if I could just work from home whenever I wanted? There's no way that it would ever be possible for a teacher to work from home."*

But clearly, I never saw 2020 coming. It hit us all like a freight train, wildly off its tracks. In the beginning of March, we began to hear rumors about this virus that was emerging in parts of the world. My husband had suggested that we buy medical-grade masks to have around, just in case, since he'd read some article online about how the virus may start to impact Americans as well. Again, I'd laughed, thinking that sounded truly insane and that there was no way we'd ever have a use for such a thing.

We were scheduled to host parent teacher conferences the week of March 13, which always overloaded my anxiety because I would get so stressed out talking to parents. This school year had been extremely challenging, and I knew that there were bound to be some conversations that would leave me with sleepless nights. In the midst of prepping for this event, rumors began to fly around the school that we may not be able to shake hands at our conferences. What? Was this some cultural sensitivity practice (we'd been having a lot of training on that lately)? Was this virus thing for real? I didn't know how to make heads or tails out of that announcement.

Friday was rapidly approaching, and I started to notice my administration running through the halls, looking haphazard and disheveled, which was absolutely abnormal. We began to receive emails from our district administration to let us know that we would be shutting down after our spring break and would not be returning for two full weeks. My students were at P.E. class, and I had just found out that we had until the end of the day to send kids home with whatever they would need, make sure that they were emotionally prepared to go home, and prepare lesson plans in advance for post-spring break.

I frantically ran to the copier, which was inevitably jammed thanks to the overflow of co-workers trying to squeeze in a few last copies to send home with their kids. The kids returned, sweaty and filled with joy, to a teacher whose face was lined with panic (although she tried to hide it well). There was a list of things on the board to take home: notebooks, some reading and writing activities, pencils, whiteboard, whiteboard marker, math book, iPad, and a classroom library book. Yes, you heard me right, my precious classroom library books which I had purchased with my own money. The prized possessions that I *never* allowed students to take home because I knew that they would be lost and never seen again.

After we had loaded up the students' backpacks, we spent the last fifteen minutes of our school day sitting in a circle, having a class meeting to tell students that we wouldn't be able to come back to the school for two weeks. I don't know if you've ever seen an eight year old during March, but they get quite excited about no-school days. Half the class erupted in joyous laughter, and immediately I had to do everything I could to keep myself from losing my sanity. The other half, however, realized the depth of what I was telling them. These were the students whose homes weren't necessarily a place they wanted to be for an entire day. School is a sanctuary for these kids. While we want to believe that all parents can provide for their children the way that my upper middle-class white family could do, that just isn't reality.

For some of my students, two weeks at home meant two weeks alone. No friends, no family, nobody to talk to. For others, this meant two weeks without a guaranteed meal. And for some, this meant two weeks of being home with a parent who didn't treat them with the respect they deserved. This meant two weeks being deprived from a trusted adult who they could share each day with, knowing that person valued them and wanted to see them each day. And knowing that was truly devastating. The students left for home; some in tears, some jumping and screaming. I began to dream of my nice little two-week vacation, thinking about all the fun things I was going to do with my friends now that I had a little extra time on my hands.

We weren't allowed to go back into our school building until the restriction was lifted, so I took a little extra time this particular afternoon to pack a few things up, making sure that I had my computer and a few other essentials. A couple of co-workers and I decided to celebrate by meeting up at a local bar to have a few drinks. Several who were invited decided to ditch at the last minute so that they could squeeze in a few extra minutes to themselves during their break. My husband, two coworkers, and I laughed over cocktails for the next two hours. We literally had no idea that this would be our final in-person interaction with people for months. Had we known, I think I would have ordered the extra cosmo.

March felt like a whirlwind. The news became bombarded by this new virus and it became quickly apparent that we had no business being outside of our home. Our administration reminded us that our expected return date had now shifted to April 8, although we should plan for an extended stay at home order. We watched as business after business shut down, except for the essentials like the grocery store. Eric's downtown job had officially gone remote until further notice, so we made the decision to adopt a dog since we'd both be home all day, at least for a while.

We'd looked and looked online for a dog, but how much really can you learn about a pup online? We saw this amazing black lab mix online who seemed to exactly fit our needs, and we waited and waited for her to become available. She had been living with a foster family, but was reserved to be adopted by someone else. Now, just to give you context, I had been the new bride who would lay on the couch asking her friends just to send her a picture of their cute dogs because I was so obsessed with the idea of being a dog mom. I would tear up when I'd browse these online ads, and my husband would give me grief because every time we saw a dog, I'd start making this squealing noise because they were so darn cute.

So, finally, after three years…. He agreed. During a pandemic. When we both would be home. Thank you, Covid?

We had given up on this pup named Felicity that we'd been looking at for weeks. There was no way this reservation would fall through, so we decided to make a shelter visit and commit to adopting a mystery dog. We wandered through the appointment-only shelter, and by some miracle, there she was. Felicity had been moved from her foster home to the shelter and the family that had reserved her had decided to go with a different dog. It was truly fate! I had tears of joy streaming down my face because for the first time in a few weeks I felt like there was some hope, some joy, and hopefully some sense of normalcy in raising a puppy together. It seemed like things might finally be turning around.

April 2020
Shifting on a Moment's Notice

MARCH SLOWLY MELTED INTO APRIL AND TEACHERS BEGAN GEARING up to return to school. We were slated to come back on April 1, but every staff meeting made it seem less and less likely that we would actually get to come back. If I had a dollar for every time we heard the phrase *"if and when* we return," I'd be able to retire by age 30.

April 1 came and went, as did the next expected return date of April 8. Finally, the district announced that we would not reopen for the foreseeable future. And then, all of the sudden, we were expected to be remote teachers. It wasn't like teachers got advanced notice or days of professional development to make this transition happen. We had to automatically become experts in creating online content to push out to students, learn how to create and run engaging virtual meetings with our class, and ensure that students' social-emotional needs were being met in a remote setting. All the while, we were each trying to navigate our own personal challenges at home; whether that be a spouse being laid off, a child under the age of two who struggled to comprehend where office boundaries are located, or simply being terrified that someone we love may contract this virus and die.

At this point in time, we didn't leave the house for anything. Grocery trips became less frequent out of fear that we may get sick from touching the grocery items. Walking down the street was terrifying because you didn't know if you'd get sick by just passing by another person walking their dog. Our world was in disorganized chaos, and as teachers, we were expected to somehow put our own fear and frustrations on hold to make sure that everyone else was taken care of.

But the thing is, that's what teachers do every single day. All the time. We put on a brave face each day, even when things feel impossible. A student has a meltdown and you're afraid that you're going to get punched in the throat? Put on a brave face and take care of it. A parent tells you that you're overreacting about a child jumping on a table or pulling a chair out from under you? Put on a brave face and don't take it personally. Oh, and by the way, don't forget to smile and be happy all the time, because that's what is expected of teachers in a regular, non-pandemic type of year. This transition to remote learning was no exception: Be a happy go-lucky teacher and create high-quality content with a program you've never used before... and go!

Our district had decided to use a program that allows teachers to post mini-lessons, videos, and assignments for students to view and complete. Most of us had never opened it before. My team of nine teachers attempted our best to divide and conquer the subject areas. By April 20, we were posting lessons in every subject area for students to complete. We started by creating lessons aligned with the curriculum that we used during a normal school year, hoping and praying that our students might learn something from it.

One of the greatest challenges in this transition to e-learning was training parents to use the new programs as well. Many of our district's families are English learners, which came with some unique barriers to overcome.

Barrier one: Some families were unfamiliar with technology, so we had to teach them how to use the iPad, how to navigate to specific websites or apps, and how to attend a virtual meeting. Did I mention that this all happened over the phone? If you've ever tried learning another language, you immediately can see the difficulty in having this as a phone conversation. When you don't understand the basics of a new language and someone who doesn't speak your language at all is trying to teach you challenging academic vocabulary without pictures, comprehension can feel like an impossible task.

Barrier two: Internet. Some of our families are low-income families who may not have access to internet connection during a regular school year. I was extremely proud of our district for going out of their way to connect families to hotspots and problem-solving ways to get kids connected to e-learning. All I can say is *All Hail the Community Schools and Technology Departments!*

Barrier three: Working from home. At this time, child care was not really an option for most people. Teachers were trying to entertain their own children during virtual appointments and parents were doing the same! Not to mention that as expectations for work completion continued to increase for students, the expectation for parent observation and follow-through also increased significantly. Who would have imagined that parents actually have to work during the work day?

Barrier four: Behavior. Teachers around the country stood by and watched as some parents encountered behaviors they had never seen before in their children. Children are not always motivated to learn, and it actually takes a huge amount of adult support to get many of them to try, to complete work and not rush through it, and to have the stamina to make it through long periods of time without breaks. I mean, can you blame kids? Playing is 1,000,000 times more fun than having to do educational work! Everyone knows that.

Facebook and Twitter erupted during the first few months of the pandemic with parents beginning to recognize the complexity of the job of teaching. Some people had the disposition that teaching was kind of like a baby-sitting gig with a little extra work to plan lessons and stuff. Little did they know that teachers are also cheerleaders, nurses, social-emotional specialists, peacemakers, entertainers, and oh yeah, teachers.

Parents, I want you to realize that this chapter is not meant to be a hit to parents. One thing that I have always appreciated about a lot of parents is that even the most stressful parent-teacher conversations are a result of passion for their children. Parents want their kids to be okay; to be successful and to be happy. Parents advocate for their kids' best interest, even though sometimes it may come from a one-sided angle.

In March and April, teachers everywhere saw what parents were going through, and we have to admit, it felt pretty good to be appreciated for once. It felt good to know that we don't suck at our job during the school year because kids are distracted or don't want to do work. It felt validating to know that parents who know their child best had some of the same struggles that we do, and that parents who shrugged off classroom behaviors finally got to see what those behaviors looked like.

Historically, parents haven't been in the classroom. Parents rush their kids to school, hoping that they get them there all in one piece and make it to their own stressful jobs. Parents trust that the professionals who entered the workforce to help children learn and grow will support their child throughout the school day. They trust that if something were to go wrong or that there was a concern, the trusted professional would let them know.

Teachers teach because they love working with kids. That's it. It energizes us to see kids succeed and see them thrive. It brings us joy to watch a kid have that "lightbulb" moment, and it is the essence of why we do what we do. My hope is that parents who may never have realized the value in what teachers do for their child might just appreciate the extra things they do for your children, that you might just listen a little closer if the teacher expressed frustrations or concerns, and that you might just say thank you to the people who work in your district. They love your child and want what's best for them too... make sure they know that you are aware of it.

May 2020
"Essential" Worker

THERE'S A LITTLE COMEDY IN LOOKING BACK TO THE PRIMITIVE nature of our class meetings and lessons in April and May of 2020. Our number one goal was to provide families with *some* sort of support as their children navigated a new level of responsibility for the first time. We were hosting a few meetings a week, sometimes 1-1 with students who had high levels of anxiety or behavioral needs, sometimes playing games with our whole class. I sure advanced quickly in hosting virtual scavenger hunts! I think it would have been easy to look at e-learning during the end of the 2019-2020 school year and think, "Wow, teachers had it so easy."

The truth is, it was heartbreaking to be a teacher in May. It was so evident that these kids were not growing, not learning at the capacity they would in a normal school setting. And there was nothing we could do about it.

This school year has been one of the most challenging I've ever had. I've only been teaching for seven years, but this was one that seriously made me question whether I could ever retire in this profession. My class was composed of many students who were in the problem-solving process to receive special services. This isn't an unusual process for teachers to go through, but my challenge was that I was trying to support eight students out of eighteen to get what they really needed.

When we were in person, I was filling out behavior charts all the time, collecting writing and math samples, managing data, communicating with special services—meaning extra support at school, attending meetings 3-6 times per month to prove and document that these students needed more than what they were getting. I was so frustrated because there were so many instances where the red tape held us back from making progress.

For the first six months of school, I was so stressed out that I actually started having physical body reactions to the levels of stress I was under. It felt like I was constantly trying to walk through a hurricane. As soon as I'd make a little progress, I'd fly backwards and fall flat on my butt. I'd heard numerous times that "You're doing an amazing job. You're collecting the data that we need, and I think these kids will get there. But unfortunately, you probably won't see it come to fruition until next school year." It was excruciating, and yet, I knew it had to be done.

I say all of this because I had put 110% of my heart and soul into modifying every single aspect of our school day to meet the needs of these diverse kiddos. Then e-learning started and all of that was washed away. Everything I had worked for, flushed down the toilet. I didn't know if my data would even be valid for the following school year. I didn't know if these kids would ever qualify for services because data collection is a multi-month long process. I didn't know if my students would be able to access the programs that we were using, let alone if they could complete any of the assignments that I assigned to them. It was gut-wrenching to see that the kids who generally did well in the classroom would complete the assignments (and sometimes even they struggled on them!) and the students who I had supported so closely in the classroom slowly disappeared off the face of the earth.

Some of those students never attended class meetings, the one social opportunity they had during the week; never attended Tier 3 services with the reading or math specialist who also had been pouring so much time into creating content and lessons at these students' ability level; and never completed assignments that had been posted.

I knew that these kids would have such a big gap of knowledge going into their next grade level and I had absolutely no control over it. Time was barreling ahead and I was trapped in my house with nothing but my thoughts.

Finally the school year came to an end, and we finished strong with a school car parade. I donned my coveted chicken hat and decorated my car with a big, beautiful sign. It was the first time I had seen any of my co-workers in months, and it was a gorgeous sunny day. It felt like the perfect way to wrap up an extremely challenging year with my class, although there was something oddly empty about it.

In a normal school year, we get to finish the year by having class celebrations. The previous year, students dressed in their finest outfits for our award ceremony. They got to dance down the red carpet runway to receive their individualized award that their classmates and teachers had voted on. It was something memorable and magical.

But in 2020, there was no runway. There were no hugs goodbye or closure with classmates and teachers. Instead, there was a slideshow presentation with their name on it and a drive-by waving ceremony to wish them well. It felt like Covid had robbed us of something really special, and it left us with so many questions about what school would look like in the fall.

Summer 2020
The Calm Before the Storm

I HAVE TO ADMIT, ONE OF THE GREATEST PERKS OF THE TEACHING profession is that you get to have your summers off. My family who works in the business world often tell me that it's just not fair, to which I always respond, "Well, you can still become a teacher!" This summer was no exception for me, I was very much looking forward to spending time with my new doggie, catching some rays, and reading books because I *finally* had time to read.

I spent the bulk of my June learning about exotic animals and polygamy with *Tiger King*, how desserts and competition intertwine in Britain in the *Great British Baking Show*, and rewatching the antics of a quirky teacher nerd like me in *New Girl* for the 15th time.

July, however, started to become its own unique beast. We had been quarantining in our home together for approximately four months now and were completely sick of anything involving a screen and were maybe even a little sick of each other too. My husband and I spent a lot of time walking the dog (I think she was up to about four walks per day), and I took every opportunity possible to be outdoors in a safe environment. I was sick of my house, sick of my lack of a routine, and sick of Covid.

One beautiful thing that came out of my quarantine misery is that I got to know my neighbors in a way that I would never have expected to in a normal year. We live in a townhome neighborhood, so we are close enough to our neighbors to be able to chat from our deck. Since my next-door neighbors had also been quarantining, not to mention that they quarantined with kids under two, they also spent a lot of time seeking refuge in the sun rays on the patio deck. I am an extrovert and I love to chat, and so we often would spend hours sharing about all the excitement of our lives pre-Covid. It was so refreshing to have the chance to get to know people who were not in our immediate household and to be able to do it in a safe way. We started to build friendships that may not have ever developed had we not been forced to spend time on the balcony together, and for that, I am extremely grateful.

The last few weeks of summer are always a busy time for teachers, with a buzzing excitement for the beginning of a new school year. There's always lots to do: plan the perfect classroom theme, get everything from name tags to folders labeled, prep and plan; the list goes on and on.

In the spring, we had seen school districts across the country with limited resources abandon any type of online learning plan. Others drove paper packets of activities to the homes of their students on a weekly basis. Some districts, like ours, created a crisis remote plan that required teachers to throw together a conglomerate of ideas and content to push out to students in hopes that they would learn something. Psychologists, educational specialists, and educators everywhere recognized quickly that this was not a sustainable model for schools to use in the 2020-2021 school year. Kids were already struggling with having limited routines, limited social interactions, and limited input and output of knowledge, and there were going to be some huge gaps in learning that would need to be addressed moving forward into the new school year.

A sense of anxiety, worry, and fear swept over the country as district administrators started devising a variety of plans that they would implement in the upcoming months. A new set of expectations and guidelines were released that would influence and change these plans on a moment's notice. Each district was responsible for making their own decisions; and I have to say, I don't envy administrators this school year at all. I think they were faced with an impossible job, and not knowing the long-term impact of any one plan would be extremely stressful and challenging. They had drastically different input from parents, teachers, other administrators, students, and other stakeholders that would need to be taken into account as plans were devised and executed.

Some schools decided to pilot hybrid learning, where part of the school day included in-person instruction and the remainder was conducted virtually via Zoom or other video platform. Our state still had strict guidelines about in-person instruction, so many schools like ours created remote learning plans.

In mid-July, our district made the decision that teachers would need to plan on working full contract hours from the school building, regardless of whether the students were in-person or remote. By the end of July, our district made the announcement that we would not be returning to any in-person learning for several weeks and we would be conducting Zoom classes from home. It was unknown when we would return to in-person learning, but teachers needed to be prepared for that moment when it happens. They called this work-from-home teaching plan the "Remote 2.0 Plan," which would look drastically different from our Crisis Remote Plan in the spring. Teachers recognized very quickly that this summer was not going to end with a stress-free anticipation for the new school year.

August 2020
New Year, New Expectations

Remote Learning Buzz Word	Textbook Definition	Real Definition
Synchronous live instruction	Students will join their teacher and classmates on Zoom for a lesson.	This class is taught on Zoom. You should be there, but we understand if you're not.
Asynchronous instruction	Students will work independently online at a time that is most conveniently for the family.	This is a lesson, video, or activity that is posted on our online platform. Complete it at your earliest convenience. If you don't want to complete it, that's okay. It's not graded.
Remote Learning	An alternative for in-person instruction.	The first ever work-from-home experience for teachers. Parents will be in charge of classroom management while working full-time from their homes and teachers will become on-screen cheerleaders.
Zoom	The online video chat platform that allows teachers and students to connect for virtual lessons and allows opportunities for group work through the use of breakout rooms.	The online video chat platform that allows teachers to be present in their students' homes. It allows students to have a "fun" experience by changing their background and gives them more opportunities to learn with their teacher in a virtual classroom!
Attendance	Any form of attendance will be accepted. Students will not be marked absent if they did not complete an assignment. If they make up an asynchronous assignment on a later date, the teacher will mark them present for the day that was previously marked absent.	Students will be counted present if they try to log in to a Zoom class or type a period on a discussion post online. No need to actually attend Zoom class or complete an assignment at grade-level quality!

R EMOTE 2.0 WAS GOING TO INCLUDE UP TO FIVE HOURS OF VIRTUAL instruction, including 2.5 hours of synchronous live instruction over Zoom, which was a program that our school had not used prior this school year. These were the recommendations from the state of

Illinois, and it was significantly higher than what was expected in the spring. The details for this plan were released on August 7, and the school year was going to begin on August 19. That left teachers with just under two weeks to learn how to use Zoom, create a ton of content to upload correctly on Schoology, find activities to lead over Zoom class, and learn all the new expectations set forth by the district. Needless to say, teachers had a lot to accomplish in a very short amount of time.

I think the biggest elephant in the room is that remote learning just simply does not compare to in-person learning. It's easy to promise families on paper that it's going to be the same experience as their kids have had in the past, the only difference being that it is conducted in a virtual setting. But when push comes to shove, remote learning is just not equitable for all children. It doesn't allow for students to engage and interact with their peers in the same way as a classroom does. It isn't easy for a teacher to just take the lesson plan that they used in the past and convert it to an online format. It doesn't allow students who need services like language, math, and reading to get their interventions in the same capacity. Remote learning is extremely challenging for all parties involved, and I think it's important for us to recognize that. All that being said, remote learning was our reality. Teachers had to make this work, and we had to do it well because our district had promised a lot of things to the families of our students.

Even though there were a lot of things to figure out to make these promises a reality, our school district worked tirelessly to make sure that all of our families had access to the materials they needed to have a successful remote learning experience. Each student from K-8 was assigned an iPad or Chromebook to keep at home, and families that had limited internet access were provided with a hotspot so that they could have internet. They also hosted many parent information sessions via Zoom to help parents who speak a variety of languages to be able to access and learn about the content that their children would be using during the school year. The school provided an incredible amount of supplies, such as scissors, paper, notebooks, and manipulatives so that all families had access to every material that would be needed at the start of the school year. They also provided and dropped off meals to families in need on an ongoing basis throughout the summer and into the school year.

While students were being well-equipped for e-learning, our district also made their best attempt to equip teachers as best as they could too. Administrators knew that there were going to be huge hurdles to overcome, including a large learning curve, for teachers to be able to do what they expected. We were provided with several training sessions, opportunities to make appointments to come to the school building to get supplies to teach from home, and orchestrated a team of people who would start putting together some of the content that we would use during the first weeks of the school year.

One unique aspect of this school year that the teachers of kindergarten, third grade, and sixth grade got to experience was completing home visits to each family in the class in order to drop off a sign for them to put in their front yard and a book with a personal note. It was really special and eye opening to see where my students lived, and it gave me a unique perspective as to what their needs may be later on in the school year. Some kids lived in neighborhoods that were teeming with other children playing in their front yards. They had the ability to interact with other kids in a semi-safe way while still staying close with their family. Other students lived in neighborhoods that made me uncomfortable to get out of my car. I entered apartment buildings, sanitizing after touching each door handle, and left signs and books for these kids, hoping that nobody was going to steal them before they got it into their home.

It was really cool to be able to have kids meet their teacher for the first time, even if it was through their window. They were excited to show their new things to all their classmates, and some may not have had any other visitors since Covid had started. I felt very honored to be able to bring that little bit of joy to them.

When I got home from this adventure around town, I started crying. Eric was wondering what was wrong, and I told him how truly blessed I was feeling. There were so many challenges that had arisen for us during the pandemic so far, but we were so thankful to have three square meals a day, have a safe way to interact with others outside of our home, to have a home in a safe neighborhood that was big enough for our family to both work remotely, and most of all to have each other. Not every family that I visited that day had all of those things, and I never wanted to take them for granted.

September 2020
Growing Pains

I TOOK ON A SUMMER JOB DURING 2020 WITH A CAMP THAT I HAD previously worked for. Camp was conducted via Zoom, so I felt confident I was ahead of the game in running hour-long Zoom meetings with students. I knew how to use background music, share my screen, and do fun or silly things to engage kids. Some of my colleagues felt stressed out about how Zoom classes would function, so we spent a lot of time practicing together before the launch of our first class with students. We got to preview our class schedules and teachers immediately had some pretty significant concerns.

The requirement from the state included that students were expected to do at least 2.5 hours of live virtual classes each day and 2.5 hours of independent work time on programs like Schoology or See-Saw (grades K-2). By looking at the schedule below, it's easy to recognize that we were far exceeding the 2.5 hours of synchronous time. Students were expected to be on Zoom for between 3-4 hours and teachers were expected to be on Zoom upwards of 5-6 hours per day. Even with those concerns expressed, Remote 2.0 moved forward and teachers learned to adapt to a full school day led via Zoom.

August- September Remote 2.0 Learning Schedule

Student Schedule

Time	M-TH
7:45-8:15	
8:15-8:30	Synchronous Overview of Schedule
8:30-9:15	Synchronous help session based on need
9:15-9:45	Synchronous Class Meeting
9:45-10:45	Asynchronous mini lesson and/or synchronous guided reading group
10:45-11:15	Asynchronous mini lesson and/or synchronous guided math group
11:15-11:45	Specials
11:45-12:15	Specials
12:15-12:45	Lunch
small 12:45-1:15	Asynchronous and/or synchronous guided math group
small 1:15-2:15	Asynchronous and/or synchronous guided reading group
2:15-2:35	Synchronous Closing Meeting

Teacher Schedule

Time	M-TH
7:45-8:15	Individual Plan
8:15-8:30	Overview of schedule
8:30-9:15	Student help session
9:15-9:45	Synchronous class meeting
9:45-10:45	Guided reading Block
10:45-11:15	Guided math Block
11:15-11:45	Curriculum co-planning
11:45-12:15	Team meeting/Professional development
12:15-12:45	Lunch
12:45-1:15	Guided math Block
1:15-2:15	Guided reading Block
2:15-2:35	Closing meeting

The first weeks of school were really spent focusing on training students and families how to use the new programs and learning the new expectations. Students no longer had as much free choice time and they were "expected" to be on Zoom calls with their teacher and complete asynchronous work when they were not on calls. For us, it went about as well as we expected, with a few growing pains along the way.

The new schedule was probably the hardest thing to get used to. It was a significant amount of time on Zoom that both students and teachers were just not accustomed to. This schedule required that teachers schedule students to attend either AM or PM classes for math and reading. This was designed to accommodate parent schedules, which sounds great, but it was really complicated and challenging for planning purposes. You see, teachers are trained to differentiate their lessons to meet struggling students' needs or to challenge advanced students. Our administration wanted us to continue doing that within these guided times, but the new challenge was that parents of students with similar needs often didn't sign up for the same times. We had to find a way to teach the same content in a way that was accessible for students across a broad spectrum of levels, and we had to find ways to make it engaging and interactive.

The other problem with this model was that due to the nature of the pandemic in the fall, there was no end of the year testing taken. Combine that with the fact that many students had limited success or attendance with end-of-the-year content, and you've got zero data to base your decision making off of as a teacher. Prior to the start of the school year, we did get the opportunity to converse with the kids' previous teacher, but many of those conversations included phrases like, "I just don't know how accurate that is," "They never attended a single class," or "I have no idea if they learned anything because they didn't complete any of their work." Putting together these guided reading and math groups was kind of like trying to piece together a puzzle that was missing a few pieces and the picture on the box cover was scratched out. We had to make a lot of inferences to determine what these students knew and what was going to be brand new to them.

One other aspect of e-learning that looked great on paper but proved extremely difficult was that our district tried to make lessons equitable for all students by requiring that no new information was taught during our Zoom lessons. Instead, all lessons needed to be posted to Schoology so that students could complete the work on their own timeline, meaning when their adults were able to support them and help with any questions, and our Zoom lessons were more supplementary. The reason they did this is that they were trying to accommodate working families' schedules and give them flexibility to complete the work together when possible.

It sounds like a brilliant plan that was very reasonable, but in reality, many of our students didn't always get the support that they needed to complete the tasks. Parents were managing not only their jobs, but also their family life. Some parents were juggling multiple school and work schedules, some parents were trying to make ends meet by working and entrusting their kids to a caretaker outside the home. Some parents struggled with depression, anxiety, and frustration. It's not hard to see that the pandemic took a huge mental health toll on families across America, so the desire to stay afloat rather than spend a bunch of time double-checking their child's Schoology discussion posts makes a lot of sense. To help train parents how Schoology worked, we taught them to check for a green checkmark to show that the work was complete.

So, that's what a lot of working parents did.

I teach third grade, which means that my students are about eight to nine years old. Developmentally, kids this age are inquisitive, work hard but have short attention spans, want to please, and struggle without a routine. They also often rely on adults to help them out as they figure out what it means to complete tasks independently. For the kids in my class who had limited adult support during the school day, whatever the circumstances may have been, there were a lot of shortcuts that they figured out how to take to make it look like they were learning when really they weren't.

It did not take long for some of them to learn that to make it appear as though they completed the work that was assigned, all they had to do was open the video lesson and close it right away. Some also quickly learned that they could make it look like they posted comments on a discussion post by simply marking a period or putting the word *okay* and clicking submit, and their adult would be none the wiser.

As the teacher who spent hours and hours putting together lessons, creating slideshows to guide supplementary lesson plans, setting and reviewing expectations every single day, it was *infuriating* that kids were not doing what they were supposed to do and that really we had empowered them to do it. There is only so much that a teacher can do to support a student who doesn't want to do their work from one side of a screen. The truth is, we really had to depend on parents to step in and help with managing the work completion and the attendance because we literally had no way to make sure that it happened otherwise.

Parents who were struggling to support their children because of difficult or conflicting work schedules, parents who dealt with temper tantrums, or parents who were disinterested in school also grew increasingly impatient with teachers too. We were required to continue reaching out to identify any barriers that may keep students from attending classes or completing work. Our objective was always to approach absences or work completion from a perspective of problem-solving rather than accusation. The message continued to be that, "We all want to solve the problem, so what can we do to support you to make that happen?"

There were some parents who dodged phone calls, didn't respond or open emails, or even marked teacher emails to go directly into their trash can. It's understandable, especially if you are someone who's fighting every day to help your family in whatever capacity you can. Teachers and administrators are human too. We have empathy towards others and have first-hand experience responding to the needs of others. However, it is still in my professional description to make sure that the educational needs of a student are prioritized during the school day. That means that I had to reach out continuously to families that I knew were struggling and continue to prod them with, "What can I do to help?" and a lot of times, neither of us knew the answer.

We both watched helplessly as the child continued to flounder, and unfortunately, both recognize the outcome that there is a possibility that child will struggle or even fall behind. It felt especially frustrating for me when I would reach out to a parent and finish our conversation feeling like we were on the same page and had a plan to move forward, but within a matter of two to five days I watched the same pattern of behavior return and continue.

In these instances, it was so hard to compose myself and not lose it on the kids. In my mind, I continually thought, *"Come on kids! It's that simple… use this fool-proof schedule that I created for you, set timers so you don't miss class, COME to class, and complete your work when you are not on Zoom!"* It's almost comical now to reflect on that mindset because these kids are literally eight years old. Most of them probably have not had to maintain their own routines or be in charge of being on time to any event ever in their life before. In the past, when they've worked on school work, there was an adult to 1) make sure they sat down to do the work *and* 2) watch them to make sure that they complete it. Many of my students were navigating their e-learning on their own because parents were working or entrusted their eight-year-old to follow those directions on their own.

Again, not a hit on parents, but I think it was eye-opening to see that many parents had no idea what a typical third grade student is capable of. As adults, we often forget that learning how to write in complete sentences, solving story problems, and managing our own time are skills that kids have to acquire and practice. It's not something that just comes naturally. There are developmental milestones that are established for each age, and without being trained what those milestones are, we forget that sometimes we set expectations far beyond what kids are able to do developmentally.

That's a big part of why teachers are evaluated on their content-area knowledge and their ability to differentiate. We are trained to use exemplars to show what typical writing samples look like, we have grade-level professional development for the curriculum so that we know what is appropriate to teach or ask students to produce at their level of development.

It became quite apparent to teachers that the type of work we were requiring of students was really beyond their developmental level. Research shows that students are more successful when they get to ask questions and experience the information that's being taught rather than have it spewed at them by a teacher. Online learning doesn't allow for that type of learning the way an in-person classroom does. Almost all of my lessons were teacher-led, and there was very little interaction between students.

I started the day with a morning meeting, which allowed the students to greet one another, share their answer to the question of the day, and go over the schedule together. This was really the only interaction they had with their peers. Eventually, I got brave enough to test out using breakout rooms so that kids could discuss with each other without cross-talk.

It was extremely intimidating at first because there is no way for the teacher to monitor what is happening in a breakout room unless you are in the same room. I started small by giving students a prompt question then gave them two minutes to share with a partner in their breakout room. I mean, what could go wrong in two minutes? At this point, the prompts were very basic and were often centered around sharing about their personal life or favorite things rather than educational topics. And it worked, for a while. Just like in your regular classroom, it takes time to build up routines and stamina and trust. I do feel quite blessed that I had a group of very respectful and genuinely kind third graders during the pandemic year. My experience using breakout rooms was more smooth than most because I knew that I could trust my students and I was very intentional to make sure I was part of their conversations and keeping them on-task.

Once we finally felt like we were in a good groove and that families knew the schedule and routines, our district decided to require MAP testing. I can understand why this decision was made: We had no data from the end of the 2019-2020 school year. Kids in the problem-solving process were at a standstill, we didn't know if students had lost a lot of knowledge due to the crisis learning plan, and we always take these tests in the spring.

This brought about an insane amount of anxiety for teachers because it was truly unprecedented to take this test in a virtual setting. It is a very high-stakes test that can determine placement for classes, and there are some very specific guidelines that we have to follow while administering the test. To throw another wrench in the mix, the district was trying to accommodate working families by providing in-person testing by appointment only, and they had the flexibility to complete it during the morning or the afternoon on Monday-Friday.

This was another situation that seemed very reasonable on paper, but was an absolute nightmare to make it happen. Teachers had to find a way to communicate to parents of all languages that there was very important testing happening over Zoom or in-person, how to sign up for in-person testing (not to mention that they didn't have to sign up for in-person), what the schedule was, and make sure that the student iPads were prepped and prepared on time for the test.

If your child is testing **IN PERSON AM**	If your child is testing **IN PERSON PM**	If your child is testing **IN PERSON TOMORROW**	If your child is **testing at home** on Wednesday

8:15-9:00
 	
Help Desk/
Independent Work
   Help Desk Zoom
   Meeting
 	
*Be at school prior to 9:00 for testing!
	8:15-9:15
	
	Help Desk/
	Independent Work
	   Help Desk Zoom
	   Meeting
		8:15-9:15
		
		Help Desk/
		Independent Work
		   Help Desk Zoom
		   Meeting
			8:15-9:15
			
			Help Desk/
			Independent Work
			   Help Desk Zoom
			   Meeting

9:00-10:30
 	
MAP MATH testing
	9:15-9:35
	
	Morning Meeting on ZOOM
	   Mrs. Schwickerath's
	   Zoom Meeting
		9:15-9:35
		
		Morning Meeting on ZOOM
		   Mrs. Schwickerath's
		   Zoom Meeting
			9:15-9:35
			
			Morning Meeting on ZOOM
			   Mrs. Schwickerath's
			   Zoom Meeting

10:30-2:15
 	
Independent Work/
Take a break
	9:35-1:00
	
	Independent Work/
	Take a break
	
	*Be at school by 1:00 for testing
		9:35-2:15
		
		Independent Work/
		Help Desk
		   Help Desk Zoom
		   Meeting
			9:35-2:15
			
			Independent Work/
			Help Desk
			   Help Desk Zoom
			   Meeting

2:15-2:35
 	
Closing Circle on Zoom
   Mrs. Schwickerath's
   Zoom Meeting
	1:00-2:35
	
	MAP MATH testing
		2:15-2:35
		
		Closing Circle on Zoom
		   Mrs. Schwickerath's
		   Zoom Meeting
			2:15-2:35
			
			Closing Circle on Zoom
			   Mrs. Schwickerath's
			   Zoom Meeting

This is an example of just one day's schedule for my class of third grade students. Administrators were responsible for managing the in-person student testing, but teachers became responsible for managing the students who were testing in-person, testing online, or were not testing on that day.

I had one spreadsheet to comb through to find out when and where these students were testing and make sure that it was easily communicated to the parents so that they weren't confused. I also had to make sure that the students knew what to do since many of them were navigating this new schedule on their own. We practiced over and over how to find the schedule, how to read the schedule, and set up timers so that they didn't miss anything on their schedule. On Schoology, I had to post four very different schedules for students to follow and somehow track if kids made it to their correct location and if they completed their tests.

Managing schedules was really just the tip of the iceberg though. Technical difficulties caused a lot of problems for my class because my Zoom account preferences did not allow them to share their screens. I didn't have the updated version I needed, so the parents had to try to help the student find very specific settings on their iPad while I gave verbal directions and visual directions to even access the test. I had no way to see if they were clicking the right buttons or accessing the right website, and it was infuriating. Only about half of my class was even able to access the test on the first two testing days while we figured out the technology kinks.

The test itself is known to be extremely challenging, and it proceeds to get harder as the student progresses through the test. It is meant to give clear data about a child's ability level without any adult support, so the directions state that adults cannot read or support the child to solve any problem on the test. As the teacher, it can be heartbreaking to watch kids struggle through 1-2 hour long tests because they don't know how to read or solve a question, but we know that it is the only way to get the most accurate data. I think it was a first for many of my students' parents to see them struggle in this way and have no ability to help them. I don't blame parents for doing so, but there were many parents who did read and even answer questions for their children on this test. When the results were finally posted, much of the data was not accurate because the child received help from an adult or the child guessed through most of the test so that they could log off of Zoom and go play.

As the teacher, looking at these results was so frustrating. Sure, it gave a good enough amount of baseline data to make a guided reading group, but I couldn't even count on the data to be correct. The intention of the test is to make accurate informed decisions about student learning and we couldn't even do that! It honestly felt like such a waste of time and an extremely unnecessary amount of stress to go through for very little payout.

Shortly after administering this test online, the district shared their plan to evolve into a hybrid-learning model starting in October-November. This shift now became at the forefront of every teacher's mind because we knew that everything was about to change drastically, and that there was so little time to make it all happen.

September 2020
Breaking Point

I HAVE ALWAYS BEEN A PERSON WHO STRUGGLES WITH HIGH-FUNCTIONING anxiety. I have always been "the girl with the plan" who needs to know what is happening, when it's going to happen, and how long it's going to last. However, in September, for the first time in my life I started to have real anxiety attacks. They were sudden and they were brutal. My husband watched as I would end each day in tears, sobbing about how stressed out I was. Oftentimes I came close to vomiting because my stomach was so tied in knots. I felt like the entire world was collapsing in on me and that I could not make it through another day of teaching. One time in particular, I was paralyzed by my anxiety and I literally could not stand. I lay crumpled in a heap for two hours in the fetal position on the floor, overcome by feelings of failure and fear. I was unable to breathe, unable to move, and unable to control my thoughts.

In addition to the anxiety attacks, I had developed plaque psoriasis all over my body which I found out were caused by stress. It is a condition that I will now live with for the rest of my life that is caused by a weakened immune system and can be impacted by external triggers like stress. My job had literally caused my body to be under attack, and that was when I knew enough was enough.

This level of stress and anxiety about my job was going to seriously impact my mental health and that there was no way I could continue living this way. We were only two months into the school year, and I had to get help or I would not be able to continue teaching. I had started to seriously wonder if I was even a good teacher, if I should ever have pursued this profession. I began looking into other professions and started making plans for how I could them happen. At one point, I thought about becoming a naturalist who worked at the botanical gardens. That dream was short-lived because I quickly realized that I wouldn't enjoy being outside in the hot summer months in the midwest. Then I moved on to the idea of opening a bakery. I loved to bake, but I had never really pursued it before. I started practicing how to make frosting roses on cakes, but again, quickly realized that there was no immediate future for me in that field either. So, while continuing to dream, I recognized that I was trapped in this profession that felt thankless and hopeless. I decided that I would push through one day at a time, and if push came to shove, I would put in my resignation and we would figure out a way to live off of a single income.

I also started to realize that what I was experiencing was a type of trauma. The level of stress I was living with was not healthy, so I began to humor the idea of working with a counselor. I was very nervous because I'd never asked for help in that way before. I was ashamed and wasn't sure what my husband or family would think of me. I really did feel like a failure, but I knew that what I was doing to cope wasn't working and that I needed professional support. I approached Eric one night, yet again sobbing, and he told me that I had his full support to work with a counselor. He would even join me if that's what I wanted. His response was better than I could have dreamed of, and so we began to look for counseling services together.

October 2020
Just Surviving

ONCE WE ENTERED OCTOBER, TEACHERS WERE GIVEN THE OPTION TO work from the school building rather than our home offices in order to prepare our classrooms for the upcoming hybrid-learning model. For me, this was a huge improvement from working at home. I love to spend time with my family, but it was so difficult to run Zoom classes with shared internet since my husband was also working from home. I had also felt extremely sad, depressed, angry, frustrated, and worst of all, lonely. I had not visited or seen people other than Eric for months, and we are usually the type of people who would get together with friends or family almost every weekend prior to the pandemic.

At home I had the same routine every day: Wake up, walk the dog, make coffee, teach, work out, make dinner, watch TV, go to sleep. I learned early on in the pandemic that if I didn't take care of myself and get dressed like I normally would that I would be lethargic and find myself in an ugly state of mind. If I didn't work out or engage my body in some kind of physical activity, I would find myself sore and burnt out by about 5:00. Some teachers were all about wearing yoga pants, not washing their hair, and wearing no makeup, but for me, maintaining some kind of normalcy was my only saving grace from going into total insanity.

Our building was only allowed to have 50 visitors at a time, but there was only a core of about 15-20 teachers and administrators who spent their time in the building at this point. Every day, I got to see a few of my coworkers and say hello. While that seems like such a small thing, it was such a big deal. It was the first time anything felt normal in seven months, and this small group of teachers were there because many of them were seeking the same thing I was. We needed a place to work and a place to be our home. We needed to interact together and laugh together, which was something I felt like I hadn't done in forever. For a few small moments each day, before all the Zoom calls and during our 15 minute lunch, I actually felt a little joy in the midst of a lot of darkness. Only one other teacher from my hallway decided to return at this time, but we would stop and greet each other every day. We'd smile and laugh, we'd help each other and support each other, and almost every day we ate lunch together. We actually talked about something other than the pandemic; something other than Zoom, Schoology, or social justice. It was a breath of fresh air and is a moment that I will hold dear for the rest of my life.

Every minute that I wasn't on Zoom or having one of these treasured moments was spent planning and calculating all the logistics of making a classroom functional with the guidelines that the CDC and our school district had put in place. Never before had we needed to socially distance students within a classroom, and figure out a model of instruction that didn't allow for students and teachers to be within six feet of each other. This was an entirely different beast, and it was going to take a lot of time to figure out all the miniscule details for how the classroom could even work.

And after having spent nearly eight months in our homes protecting ourselves and our families from the invisible virus, it felt quite intimidating to think about how we would be able to have a functioning classroom, even at limited capacity, if we couldn't share any supplies or be close to each other. Not to mention that there would be a high number of people occupying the same space, which was something we hadn't experienced since pre-pandemic times. Many people, myself included, were so nervous to contract the virus or bring it home to our vulnerable families.

At this point in time, it was suggested that the virus could be passed on surfaces. This meant no shared supplies in the classroom, which is absolutely contrary to the philosophy of our district in prior years. We had been trained that shared supplies were equitable so all students had access to supplies, regardless of their family's income level. To allow for social distancing, we were required to put our desks into straight lines, six feet apart, all facing the same direction. Again, this was a significant shift in mindset about what's the best teaching practice, so it had a major impact on the way our lessons would be taught and facilitated.

Teachers had no idea what kind of supplies students would be able to bring with them to school, not to mention whether it was even safe to cross-contaminate supplies between home and school or vice versa. That meant we had to be prepared for kids to enter our classrooms with absolutely nothing, so we would need to supply it all for each student individually.

School leadership teams meticulously created plans for how students would take bathroom breaks, developed checkout systems for exiting the classrooms, and fine-tuned eating or drinking procedures. They developed a home-certification system that required parents to certify their child's health prior to entering the building for the day. All of the new safety protocols came out rapid-fire, and teachers had to relearn every procedure while processing how to communicate those new procedures to students and parents. We received a 50-page document from the district that we had to comb through to feel confident about the procedures for in-person and remote learning.

Questions constantly swirled in my mind, like, "How do I help a student who is struggling at their desk if I can't get within six feet of them? How do the students interact with each other at school? What kind of activities can we even do if we can't all touch a ball, pass out a piece of paper, or share any other types of supplies?" It all felt so over-whelming, but there was no escaping it. You had to jump on board, and quickly, or you would not be prepared for the transition. We put together video tutorials, visuals, practiced procedures collaboratively, had extra team meetings, had "coffee talks" with administration, and spent lots of additional hours on our screen to prepare while also continuing to lead several hours of e-learning on Zoom each day.

Starting October 19, all staff members were now required to work from the building in order to prepare classrooms for in-person learning. There was an array of feelings among staff members. Some were so nervous to be in person that they did not make contact with a single person in the building, except for via Zoom, and were extremely frustrated with that decision because it felt so unsafe. Other teachers, like myself, who had been in the building longer felt much more comfortable with being in the same building together, but there was now a very different work environment that we had to learn to navigate. Even teachers who once found joy in coming to work because they got to see each other started to find themselves glued to their classrooms, secluded from everyone else in the building out of necessity.

One of the hardest challenges in preparing for the transition to hybrid learning was actually the inability to meet with other teachers face to face. It was very clear from our administration that teachers should not congregate, eat, or have meetings together in the same space. We were required to be alone in our classroom with our door closed in order to remove our mask, which meant that interacting with colleagues was no longer a thing. We spent our day inside of a fishbowl, feeling like we were so close to some form of normalcy compared to our experience with working from home, yet we were so far away from life as we knew it before the pandemic. This lack of social-ization meant that teachers didn't have the opportunity outside of Zoom meetings to talk about their life, about their struggles, or even about what they were processing about this big change. We watched as each of our team members slipped into high levels of stress and anxiety, and we began to project it on each other.

All of our team meetings were very task-oriented, very serious, and felt like well spent and wasted time all at once. Each of us had a checklist of to-dos that reached the floor, and while the time to collaborate with colleagues was important, it felt unfortunate that we couldn't use that time to multitask. Our school building has between 8-10 members on a grade-level team. During a regular school year, we were split into "pods" of 4-5 teachers. Each week you would only meet with this smaller pod, and you met as a whole team maybe a couple times in a school year. In the 2020-2021 school year, we were spending 2-3 hours each week on a call with a 9-teacher team. Our team leaders were frustrated because every decision that was made would not please everyone, and sometimes we talked in circles when trying to come to a final decision because there were so many cooks in the kitchen. One team leader described it best: "This team is known for being hard-working and vibrant, but this year we are truly exhausted. People are struggling, and it feels like nobody is accounting for that." At the end of each team meeting, you could scan each person's face and see the exact same look: devastation. We were drowning, and it felt like it took every ounce of energy to even exist.

November 2020
Almost There

NEGATIVE ENERGY AND ANXIETY WERE AT AN ALL-TIME HIGH IN THE final days of preparation before in-person learning began. There was so much uncertainty as to whether the procedures and policies that were set in place during this time would be enough to counter an invisible virus, and teachers continually felt like they had no voice at board meetings.

However, one moment of joy that seemed to bring teachers out of this funk and back to life was our Fall Drive-Through Parade. I naturally dressed up in a chicken hat and covered my car with a sign that said "Don't be CHICKEN, honk if you're happy to be here!" We stood outside on a day with the most perfect weather cheering on our students and their families as they drove by in their cars. This was the first time I ever saw any of my kids outside of our Zoom class, and they were beyond excited to see me. It's a good thing I told them about my outfit, because I don't think many of them even knew who I was with my mask on. Teachers and administrators were laughing, dancing, smiling (although you couldn't see it), for the first time in what felt like an eternity. We got a glimpse of what it was like to be a real teacher again, to do the thing that we always loved to do.

Following the parade event, we spent about two more weeks prepping and preparing the classroom. A difficulty that we came across was determining which students were going to start attending in-person sessions and which students would remain remote. The elephant in the room was always a matter of equity: which students are going to receive a better education? Will the students who stay remote fall even further behind? How do we manage having in-person students, online students, *and* continue to create and push out content for all students online? Students, parents, and teachers were finally feeling like they were in a good groove with online learning. Everyone knew how to access the content, they knew the expectations, and most of them were completing their work each day.

As the news about the transition to in-person learning came out, students who learned that they would be starting in-person learning began to get very excited, and those who were staying remote were often very confused. These 8-year-olds didn't understand why other kids got to go to school and see their friends while they had to stay at home. Some parents never talked with their children about the decision that was made, which left that conversation to become my responsibility. We were trained what to say and how to say it so that the family never felt like they were making the wrong decision for their child. "Each family is making the decision that feels right for them, and there's no right or wrong decision. I'm excited to continue teaching each one of you, whether you're in-person or at home! Things are going to be different, but it's going to be okay."

Starting on November 4, students entered our building for the first time. Many felt ecstatic and overjoyed to be there, while others felt a bit overwhelmed and scared. I found myself somewhere in between. We spent much of the first day going over our procedures of how to keep each other safe and healthy, and our third graders got to tour the necessary parts of the building because they had never been there before. They would stare longingly at the playground, so I knew that I needed to make sure to check out a time for them to go outside regularly. Playing outside seems like something that kids should always have the right to do, and yet, these kids had been robbed of that experience for almost seven months. To me, it felt like there was a world that was crashing in on these kids, consuming them with fear and anger and anxiety. My job extended far beyond the curriculum this year. I was going to make learning fun, make it collaborative as much as I could. I wanted these students to feel joy again in the classroom, and overwhelmingly, I think they did. At the end of our 2 ½ hour time together, I would walk my ten students to the dismissal door and chat them up about their favorite parts of the day. My heart broke when one child told me, "I wish that we had testing here every day just so that we could be in school." Others would sigh when the clean-up bell would ring, and they would dream out loud of the day when all the students could come to school every day of the week for a full day.

In my mind, I kept thinking *in what world does a kid want to have more time in school?!* In my entire teaching career, I'd never had the experience of students telling me that they wished the school day was longer. I think it goes to show that school can be life-changing for some children. It provides a structure that they may not have otherwise at home. For some, it's a safe place with adults who treat them kindly or even give them attention. For others, it's a place where they are guaranteed a meal. And for all children, it's a place to learn how to be a good friend and develop relationships with adults and peers outside one's own family. Yes, family time is so important and special. But these kids made it so evident that they were just seeking connection; seeking a world beyond the four walls of their home. I felt exactly the same way in my home, and there were only two people there!

Other than providing a positive school experience for the in-person students, my greatest goal was to make sure that my remaining nine remote students didn't lose hope or lose interest in school. I wanted my class to feel like a collaborative community rather than two smaller classes. That was an extreme challenge, and most days, I felt quite unsuccessful at it.

After my in-person students were dismissed, I had just enough time to use the restroom before I had to hop onto Zoom with my remote kiddos. There was a wide variety of personalities in this group. It ranged from students who participated less than 1 time per day to others who wrote huge sentences on every discussion post and attended every class meeting. We spent about 30 minutes just checking in, reading a story together, and working on any missing assignments. These kids were fatigued, but even those who didn't regularly come previously in the year started to show up. They were seeking connection, and that short time frame was almost perfect for them to get what they needed. Even though some of the content during our "guided reading block" was more watered down than it was for my in-person group at times, I still held these students to the same high expectations. I knew that every single one of them could complete their tasks, write complete sentences, talk with a partner, and manage their behaviors on Zoom. They rose to the occasion, following a new schedule and changing their ingrained routines. I was so proud of them, and so thankful to the families who were making sure that their child was attending their online classes. I truly couldn't have done it alone.

During the afternoon, all students were required to join a Zoom meeting for math. I think this was such a disservice to the students because math was one of the most challenging curricula to teach in a remote setting. It was so hard to keep kids engaged, participating, and comprehending the complex nature of the lessons. Many of the lessons that were identified as our "priority standards" were actually hands-on lessons in the books. That meant that we literally had to modify everything so that kids could experience the content visually instead of physically. We would do materials pick-ups regularly throughout the school year, which often included math manipulatives (or supplies that they could move around with their hands to help them learn). Literally the day that all students received them, I would say something like "Take out your fraction strips. That's the colorful page in the bag you picked up from the school," and I'd immediately have five students who could not find the material. It was excruciating. It was also an hour long class over Zoom, and research shows that students' attention spans often only range from 5-10 minutes. We were not supposed to ever upload video lessons longer than 3 minutes because we recognized that students would click out of the lesson if it exceeded that length, and yet somehow teachers were supposed to engage students on Zoom for six times that amount of time.

For a while, I attempted guided math groups. My thought was that I would have much more success in teaching smaller groups because then kids would be able to answer questions more frequently, and they wouldn't feel so much pressure to show their work to their peers. What actually happened is that many of my students would hear the directions about what to do in their breakout room and sign off to never return. I also had many students who would randomly sign on 10-30 minutes late to class and would miss the entire lesson. Needless to say, this type of small group was great on paper but did not work in reality.

The next two weeks went by quite quickly. My students and I adapted quite quickly to the hybrid schedule and became quite fond of it. The 2 1/2 hours of in-person learning felt like enough to keep kids engaged without feeling overwhelmed. I got enough time most days to get my video lessons and content recorded and uploaded during school hours, and my class attendance and participation was probably close to 80%. Both groups seemed to be enjoying school, which to me felt like a huge win for us all.

Thanksgiving break seemed to loom over us all starting in the second week of November. Teachers, myself included, were feeling quite concerned about the number of families who may travel over the holiday and would not have the ability to quarantine after their trips. We listened as district after district in our area started to announce school closures or "flip remote" schedules for post-Thanksgiving break, but our school did not. It seemed that there was a belief that our students' families, who were mostly low income, would not travel over the holiday and that it would be the staff who travelled who would spread the virus around. If we wanted to quarantine after traveling, we would have to use our sick days or personal leave to do so. This was absolutely infuriating because it felt like our policy makers did not have any intent to require quarantine after travel. (Keep in mind, the largest city in the state was requiring a mandated 14-day quarantine after traveling outside of the state.)

I was very conflicted during this time too because my husband and I did have family who lived outside of the state. We made the decision after months of contemplation to travel on an airplane to see our family for the holiday. We knew the risks, but we also knew that it would possibly be more than two years before we would get to see some of these family members if we didn't do it. There was this overwhelming sense of secrecy within our school building, because we all knew that there would be people who would travel but nobody wanted to admit that they were taking that risk. It was all so stigmatized, and even our upper administration was putting pressure on people to forgo any plans because they would not require a quarantine and traveling would put students and their families at risk.

As the holiday approached, Eric and I went back and forth about whether we should go through with it. I spent hours in tears feeling extremely guilty over the thought of potentially spreading this deadly disease to my students. I also knew that out of my 10 in-person students, more than half were planning to travel across the country to visit relatives and that they would in turn be putting me and the other students at risk. I felt helpless, irresponsible, and heartbroken that I would have to make our immediate family miss the once per year gathering on my account.

Finally, around the 20th of November, our district announced the decision to do a "adapted pause" schedule through January 13. Teachers across the buildings celebrated because we now could make the right choice for our own families without feeling this overwhelming guilt. We didn't have to put our vulnerable family members at risk by exposing them to students and staff who had traveled over break. It was ensured that we would be able to work in our at-home environment and quarantine as needed following the major holidays. At the announcement, I cried because I felt like a weight had been lifted off of my shoulders. I still had extremely high levels of anxiety about traveling to see my own family, but at least I could make that decision without it being controlled by my job.

December: Adaptive Pause

8:00- 8:15	Morning Meeting (on Zoom)
8:15-10:45	Literacy: Reading/Writing/ FUNdations (on Zoom)
10:45-11:15	Small Group (on Zoom)
11:15-11:45	Lunch at home
11:45-12:20	Science or Social Studies (independently online)
12:20-1:20	Specials Classes (on Zoom)
1:20-2:20	Math (on Zoom)
2:20- 2:35	Closing Meeting (on Zoom)

Promptly following Thanksgiving break, students began following a new schedule called "flip remote" schedule. It basically took our in-person schedule and flipped it to a Zoom setting. Had I known that we would go from our old remote schedule to this new schedule, I would have absolutely jumped ship. The reasoning behind this new schedule was that it would be "easier for the students who were in-person to transition." Honestly, it made me wonder if these decision makers were even listening to what teachers had to say during our first experience with a completely remote setting.

From the day the new schedule came out, teachers became extremely frustrated because we could already foresee the extreme challenges that would come with a full day of Zoom for 3rd-5th grade students. We kept saying to our administration that we knew this was not best practice for students and could actually hinder learning because they would get burnt out. We had experienced this earlier in the year, when students were having a hard time managing only two or three hours of Zoom classes and online content. With the new schedule, 8 year olds were being asked to spend more than six hours on Zoom and complete up to 1-2 hours of independent content online. It felt absolutely insane, and just as we expected, our burnout rate skyrocketed over the next month and a half.

At first, the bulk of our time was spent trying to help kids and their families navigate our new online schedule. Even though it was exactly the schedule we followed at school, neither the kids nor adults were familiar with it in their homes. It wasn't uncommon for kids to come to classes anywhere from 7:45 A.M. until 6:30 P.M. and have absolutely no idea when any of their actual classes started even if they could access the schedule.

I am the type of teacher who naturally loves to be silly and do things like wearing fun hats to engage my students. But over time, in order to even get my kids to come to classes, I had to find innovative new ways to make my classes interesting. I might be entertaining at times, but I am not a YouTuber, not an Instagram influencer, or TikTok star. I am a teacher, and my job is actually to teach at some point. Educational content is not always as fun as Roblox or as funny as social media, and when kids are spending hours upon hours on these fun online platforms outside of (or even during) school hours, I didn't even stand a chance.

I felt myself sink into this state of depression and frustration over the lack of interest in my classes during Zoom class. My students who used to love having their videos on and sharing about their family or their life now were becoming zombies who came to classes only because their parents made them. Often, in my class of 18, I would only have between 6-12 even show up. Many of them arrived 30 or more minutes late and didn't even connect to audio. My screen became dark as each student started using their videos less and less, and my frustration grew when I would ask questions to students or ask them to respond in the chat or with a thumbs-up reaction and they were nowhere to be found. I learned that the only way to get some of my kids to even interact with me or the rest of the class was to continue clicking the "request to unmute" button so that they knew I was calling on them.

The hardest part of it all was knowing the amount of hours I spent outside the school day, when I felt like I had no brain left to even function with, making slide deck after slide deck to lead my classes the next day or making videos to post the upcoming week.

As time continued, many of my students stopped completing the online work altogether. To be counted present, they literally could post a period or write the word *done* as an answer to a discussion post, so that's what some of them did. Then I got to spend hours on Thursdays after school going through worthless discussion posts and quizzes to "grade" them so that I could report to parents how their children were doing and be forced to give them a grade on a report card. It was the most inaccurate and one of the most frustrating and pointless things I feel like I've done in my career. Every action that I took for work felt like I was just checking a box, and that has never been a way that I've approached my job before.

I also got quite frustrated at the parents of some of my students, but I wasn't allowed to show it. I *had* to show empathy to these families because we are in the middle of the pandemic and there was a lot going on. Their child could sign on for 2 minutes of an 8 hour school day and be counted present and it was *my* fault that they weren't learning or that they were falling behind. And if I brought it up to them that their child was missing school and falling behind, I would be met with excuse after excuse, some valid and some not.

I am an empath by nature. I take on people's burdens and I feel deeply for others. I consider it my greatest strength and greatest weakness. Writing that last paragraph makes me feel like the most heartless person in the world and feels extremely outside my character. But I don't think that I should have to leave it out of my story because it may hurt some people's feelings.

There are parents out there at every single school who do not put in the work to give their child the best chance at the education they deserve. Teachers fight and fight and fight for these kids, and often are met with combative parents who don't want to own up to their own actions. It is infuriating, mostly because it doesn't seem to reflect poorly on the parent. It is often the teacher who takes the heat, who receives the blame that their student is not achieving or has significant behavior problems. And the worst part is that our society empowers this kind of parental behavior. Society teaches us that we don't need to have respect for educators, that we don't need to teach our kids respect for people in authority.

This is a problem that has existed far before the pandemic and I fear it is a problem that will not get better over time. There are many, many parents who do everything they can for their children and teach them values and morals that will make them great human beings as they get older. I don't want you to hear that all parents are bad or disrespected by teachers. What I am saying is that for those parents that can't own up to their own mistakes and do everything they can to get their kid to school on time, get it together. Your child deserves better than that of you, and if there is a teacher telling you that your child is misbehaving, bullying, falling behind, needs to come to school, etc. that you need to consider that what they are saying is true. Not every teacher is perfect, and not every teacher has the same expectations. But overall, teachers love kids and want what is best for them. They deserve everyone on their team to be fighting for them to succeed, not just their teachers.

There were two pretty common phrases that I heard from parents when the issue of attendance or participation were addressed during our remote setting: "We had a temper tantrum and lots of frustration, so we decided they didn't need to attend today," and "I didn't realize they weren't coming or doing their work. We'll make sure that they start attending." While I can see the perspective of these responses, I had such a hard time not becoming overly frustrated with these families, especially when the issues continued day after day and were addressed 5, 10, 15 times over the course of a month. I am not a bad guy trying to accuse you of being a bad parent! If kids don't come to school and don't do their work, they actually don't learn. They don't just get information and knowledge through osmosis.

As far as temper tantrums are concerned, imagine not only having one student, but rather having 15-25 kids in one room of your house trying to complete something they don't understand or want to understand. They might get frustrated or decide there is something they would much rather be doing. You are the only adult in the room and you are not supposed to get upset or yell and you're supposed to teach them in a variety of ways because they each have drastically different needs. Also, imagine that the internet suddenly stopped working and they were all supposed to individually complete an assignment online. What would you do?

This is my reality. Every. Single. Day.

During a single school day, I have to manage the behavior, the interest level, the happiness level, the relationships, and the input of knowledge for a large number of kids. I have had things thrown at me, I've been called horrible names, I've been told that I'm stupid and not important more than once. I know many others who have been bitten, kicked, slapped, hit by children in their rage. I may have had a solid four years of college education to teach me about how kids think and develop, but I have never been trained as a social worker or a technology consultant. And I am not a parent, so I don't want to make it seem like I know everything or anything about parenting. But what I do know is that teachers who are as young as age 22 have to manage temper tantrums and find a way to get students to learn among a large group of other children. If we can manage this for 15-30 kids, it is possible to find a way to engage one child in getting their schoolwork done even if it takes an insane amount of time and patience.

Another big challenge during remote learning was that we used the "data" collected during our fall MAP testing to determine which kids should receive interventions. This is a process that schools use every single year and should be able to help serve kids who need extra support in reading, math, or English. However, due to the nature of our schedule and the type of support that could be offered online, these populations were expected to not only complete their regular amount of work and attend 6 hours of classes, but they were also expected to complete 30 minutes of intervention work on an independent online program each day after school. Teachers expressed to administration time and time again that it was too much for kids and that the ones who needed the most support were now being expected to do more work than students who could complete work independently on their own. It felt extremely backwards and honestly made teachers feel horrible assigning extra work so that they could receive "intervention," even though there was not a teacher actually supporting them.

For my class, many of the kids receiving this type of Tier 2 support were my students who never came to class and never completed any of their work. I knew that they would never log in to this program no matter how many reminders I gave to them or their parents, and there was absolutely nothing I could do about it. I also knew that there were staff members tracking the amount of usage of the program for future data purposes and that it only reflected poorly on me as their teacher if they didn't complete the assignments.

We also administered winter benchmarking tests in December. If you remember, administering this test over Zoom in the fall was one of the reasons I considered ending my teaching career. The amount of stress and anxiety it caused me was overwhelming, and I carried a sense of PTSD when they announced that we would be giving those tests again. There was really no necessity to give these tests in the winter, no state requirement. It was truly an administrative decision, which felt especially frustrating to teachers because we knew that once again the data that was provided would be inaccurate and wouldn't be useful moving forward.

However, there were two significant differences between this testing extravaganza and the prior. This time, teachers had the ability to come to the building to administer the test over Zoom rather than from their homes. Just having the ability to get technology support if needed was huge for me. I like to think I'm tech-savvy, but when it comes to high-stakes testing and the responsibility of figuring out how to solve technology problems on the fly, I have my own battles to overcome with anxiety before I'm great at problem solving. The other significant difference was that we had already given this test once virtually, and as far as I'm concerned, my class could not have had more road bumps that had to be resolved by administration or the technology gurus at school. They did a lot of the heavy lifting to determine why the online testing didn't work in the fall and made sure that the students' iPads had all the correct apps, settings, and testing information. Due to the large number of students who opted in for in-person testing and these supports that were in place for teachers during testing, all of my students were able to test successfully. I guess we can count that as a victory.

The district was heavily suggesting that staff members should not travel for the holiday season because staff were required to work at the school building starting on January 4. Once again, this put me in a very difficult position where I felt like I had to sneak around and wasn't able to determine the right choice for my family without the guilt of thinking I would get all of my students and their vulnerable family members sick. Many of my coworkers got to see their family members regularly, at a socially distanced gathering or a drive-thru parade, because they live in the area. Our family does not live close, and in the midst of the stress and loneliness that Covid-19 had put on our family as a whole, Eric and I made the decision to drive to visit my family even though we knew the risk. I spent a lot of hours going back and forth on this decision prior to the trip, stressing myself out and running my anxiety levels through the roof.

Are you sensing a theme yet? Every decision that I had to make this school year that could potentially impact my students, their families, my colleagues, or my family gave me extreme levels of anxiety. I no longer felt like I was living with high-functioning anxiety because every decision I made left me feeling panicked and paralyzed.

Now, it felt like even little decisions had become big decisions. I was constantly living in this state of fear and frustration, worried that something I decided to do was going to cause another person to get sick and die. And the message that I continued to receive from our administration was that if we didn't follow every protocol set in place and didn't hunker down in our homes that we would, in fact, get someone else sick. They would have the epidemiologist share reports and timelines that would show us exactly the days we were in person and how an infected person could get us sick and we wouldn't even know it until it was too late. It was exhausting trying to live by these guidelines, and it was even more frustrating to know that many of my friends and family members in a neighboring state were not following these guidelines.

About a month before Christmas, my aunt became a victim of Covid-19. We weren't able to attend her funeral because we were scared of Covid-19. If anything, it caused me to want to be even more cautious because now I had experienced my first personal connection with the virus. This thing that I was so scared of, getting sick and dying, was actually happening to my family and it was extremely frightening.

The worst part was that I knew that if I went to see my family that they may not have quarantined prior to our visit. Several members of the extended family were invited to celebrate Christmas together. We weren't told about these guests until we had already made the decision to come and to be quite honest, it was really hard to continue our journey there. My job made me hyper-sensitive to the impact of Covid on vulnerable persons, and again, every decision I made had an impact on the people I interact with back at school. I felt an extreme amount of stress daily, and it felt so unfair that I even had to consider not spending holidays with my family because some stupid virus could kill someone I know and love based on my actions. It was also exhausting to navigate how different people felt about the virus, constantly telling us that we were too cautious or that we worried too much.

Even though I felt high levels of anxiety during the last few months of the year, I learned how to manage my anxiety by going to therapy. I had known after my first true anxiety attack that I had to get professional help, and thankfully my husband was completely supportive of that decision. We found a therapist who was easy to talk to and who specialized in the area of anxiety. She helped me identify what my triggers were that caused the anxiety, which was the first and most important step in helping me manage it. I discovered that if my brain used the phrase "What if…" to start a thought, I was going to spiral into anxious thinking. She gave me some mindfulness tools to use when I would identify a trigger phrase, including the five-finger trick (as I like to call it) and breathing exercises that can help bring me out of anxious thinking and back to my present reality.

We talked with my husband about my anxiety, which allowed me to learn how he perceived my anxiety attacks. I used to feel shame, to feel out of control. I thought he perceived me as weak, so I didn't allow myself to talk about these deep fears that I had with him. I always held back until I learned that he never saw me as weak. In fact, he saw me as quite the opposite. He shared about how he felt helpless in the moments when I was feeling most broken and how he wished he could take away the pain or convince me to talk about what I was experiencing.

My therapist also encouraged me to journal, which I was hesitant to do at first. It quickly evolved and began to serve a much greater purpose than just self-awareness and mindful thinking. When I started writing, I started to feel a sense of freedom, of fulfillment. And what felt so bizarre at first was that teacher after teacher that I talked to would share about their experiences during this school year and they mirrored many of the thoughts and conversations that I'd had. These were colleagues, past colleagues, friends from other districts, friends from other states, and family members who were experiencing the same types of challenges as I was time and time again. I read articles and posts online about how more than 30 percent of teachers in 2020 were considering changing career paths or retiring early. My therapist shared that in the year 2020, her caseload increased by 20 or more teachers who were experiencing extreme anxiety and depression.

My story all of the sudden had relevance. I had a new mission: to share with the world the perspective of one teacher. I wanted to show myself that I could dedicate my life to doing something good this year, in the midst of all the ugliness in our world. I wanted to show Covid that it did not get to steal something so precious to me: my joy and passion for teaching. This year was absolutely hell for more reasons than one, but in some twisted way, it has empowered me to speak my truths so that hopefully others will one day be able to speak theirs.

January 2021
Everything Will Be Different

I REALLY WISH THIS PART OF THE STORY ACTUALLY STARTED WITH THE phrase "In January, everything that caused pain and suffering in 2020 disappeared." Clearly, that was not the case. But funnily enough, there was a new sense of refreshment and hope that came with the start of a new year.

Having spent time with my family over the holiday, I was quite hesitant to interact with my colleagues out of fear for their safety. Every staff member was required to be in the building, and it was almost eerie the way people seemed to avoid one another, like they had secrets to hide. I think there were probably many like me, who had made the brave and maybe stupid decision to celebrate the holiday season out of state or out of the city and were embarrassed to tell others about it. There was a feeling of shame or guilt that accompanied the decision to travel, even though in any normal year we wouldn't think twice about sharing this information with our friends and colleagues.

Every day, I entered my fishbowl classroom and led hours upon hours of frustrating, low-attendance Zoom classes. I said, "Good morning," and, "Have a good night," to people as I passed by them every day. Typically in American culture, when people say, "How are you doing?" our go-to response is a cheerful, "Good!" But the new phrase to answer this question became, "Hanging in there." The running joke actually became *why do we even ask each other this question?* You can see in every face, in every interaction that people were not fine or good, but rather that people were literally hanging on by threads. It almost started feeling like common courtesy to not ask each other about how life is because nobody had anything but negative or empty thoughts to share.

I spent a lot of my time at the school making sure that I balanced being on a screen with completing tasks around the classroom that needed to be completed before January 19, which was our expected return to in-person date. I was actually feeling quite excited because although there was a lot of exhausting work to get done in order for students to come to the building, I actually felt like a real teacher for one of the first times this school year.

I got to arrange my desks, put up bulletin boards, and cut things out. They sound like such stupid and simple things, but they are simple things that brought me joy. When my classroom finally looked like a place where students would feel happy to be, I sat at my desk and cried. I knew that the next phase was going to be challenging and that there were a lot of scary things coming my way, but I also felt hope that this might also be the last time we ever had to change schedules at the last minute. Maybe I would actually get to feel like I had taught my students something, even if it was only reading and even if it was only for two and a half hours each day.

January 19 arrived, and I had 11 students join me in the classroom during the morning. Essentially, we spent our time at school doing a morning meeting, grammar lessons, a read aloud, and a reading lesson. At 10:30, they would pack up and head home. In the afternoon, they would attend specials classes, math, and closing circle on Zoom.

This group of kids came into the classroom with such excitement to be back at school and such happiness to be able to be off of Zoom in the morning. In fact, they rarely used their iPads in the morning, and I think that they found it quite refreshing. They loved the small class setting because they got lots of opportunities to share their thinking, do partner activities with many different partners, and listen to stories that they loved.

One of the most memorable parts of our hybrid learning was that we started a Patricia Polacco reading and writing unit, and we kicked it off by learning about how her grandmother used to tell her stories by the fireplace. I decided that we were going to have "fire talks" like Patricia Polacco, and each day I would turn on the virtual fireplace on my TV screen and read one of her stories to them. They were about 15-20 minutes long, and the kids soaked in every single word. Some days, they would ask to check out her books so they could re-read the stories we'd read earlier in the week. When it was time for the unit to end, I started to put the books away and my students yelled at me! "Why do you have to put them away? They are our favorites! Can't you put them in the classroom library so we can check them out anytime?" I mean, I couldn't really argue with that, could I? So, I put out a special Patricia Polacco book box and the kids continued checking out her stories regularly through the end of the year.

My students loved this unit so much that I decided to work with our reading specialist to come up with a special video project to send to Patricia Polacco herself. She has an email on her website where students can submit an email or letter to her, and sometimes she will respond. I wanted our class to stand out because it was obvious how special her stories were to them. We put together a video montage of the kids telling her why she was important to them and what their favorite stories were. It brought me so much joy to be able to put this together and send it off to Patricia.

Unfortunately, when I went to send the letter her inbox was full, but I never told the kids that. It was still a special project to me because it showed how passionate my students could be about learning, and it was one way that I could be the best teacher I could be for them. I could cheer them on to create something meaningful, to feel proud of their accomplishments, and to teach them that to love reading is one of the most powerful and special things in a person's life.

In early January, rumors started to mill around that a vaccine would soon become available for teachers and district staff members. I was hesitant at first because I knew that so few people had received the vaccine and felt a bit like a guinea pig. I often found myself in a place of anxiety because my husband and I had just decided to start trying to have a baby and I was extremely concerned about what could happen to a potential pregnancy. I spent hours researching, talking with other colleagues, fretting over the decision. Then one night, we received an email that required us to sign up immediately or we would have to wait a long time before they would become available again. I decided to muster up the courage to get it because the risks of not getting one felt much worse than to get one. I wanted to protect myself so that I can protect my family at home and my students' families. It was pretty amazing how the culture of our school building began to drastically change after more and more staff members became vaccinated. People were still being smart and cautious, but they were not being ruled by fear that they would get sick from everything and everyone in the building. People began to seek out relationships again and there was a sense of relief that maybe someday things might be normal again.

February 2021
Hybrid In-Person Learning

HYBRID IN-PERSON LEARNING CONTINUED THROUGH THE MONTH OF February with no end in sight, which actually felt like a good thing. Students at school seemed to be figuring out how to be in a classroom setting and the remote students were getting into a good groove too. It was a bit unnerving as a teacher to have students in both settings but feel like you could commit more fully to one group over the other. We knew going into hybrid learning that there would be a sense of inequity as far as the amount of teacher-student time the remote students would get.

We spent about 30 minutes each day meeting with students in the morning, which usually consisted of a check in to see how they were doing, a share about their day so far, and a short reading lesson. We knew that some of these kids would only ever practice reading out loud during this 30 minute call, so we needed to prioritize that type of activity. For a while, it was a struggle to get all of my remote students on in the morning due to a variety of reasons, but thankfully most of my students that needed a lot of support were now participating in the in-person setting where I could give them the support they needed. I felt particularly blessed by this because there were many other teachers in our building who had only four or five in-person students and had a majority of their class online who they felt were being neglected in a sense.

The afternoons brought whole-group specials classes, math, and closing circle. I learned very quickly that students who attended in-person learning often did not care to attend afternoon classes. Since this was the only time I got to work on math with them, I noticed that students who stopped attending regularly started to have huge knowledge gaps which then deterred them from wanting to attend future classes. I started a few of these students on "attendance plans" to help their parents and myself keep track of the amount of time that these kids were missing and give them a little bit of a reward for responsible behavior. It worked for some, and for others, it was a shot in the dark. The trouble was that if parents didn't buy into the attendance reward system and encourage the child to attend at home or possibly planned family activities during at-home class times, I had no chance to get the student motivated to attend. This was something I learned to live with and tried not to take personally, even though it felt like poor attendance was something that was reflecting on my teaching ability.

Eventually, after I felt like I had burned every bridge with these families who were struggling, I decided that I had to get extra support. There had to be a place where my responsibility to track kids and parents down was passed on to a higher power.

The thing is, parent relationships really do make or break a school year. I take a lot of pride in the way that I interact with the families of my students, whether I'm voicing concerns or sharing exciting news. I am very intentional with every email, phone call, and personal interaction because I want them to know how much I care about their child. This season of the school year felt especially straining to parent relationships because for the kids that didn't participate, it was the same ol' song to these parents. They stopped listening, decided that they were going to do what they were going to do, and I was just bringing them down or making them feel like a crappy parent. And a lot of the time, I felt like I was making them feel like a crappy parent! I can recognize that e-learning is extremely challenging for many of the families that I have to communicate with the most often. They may not have been able to send their kids to in-person school because they had to work during the day or had other responsibilities at home or even outside the home. They may not have the transportation, the supplies, you name it. I recognized that these families needed support desperately, that these kids needed adult support even more so, and that all I could do to stop the system was send an email or phone call that said, "Hi, this is so and so from the school. Please make sure you review the schedule so your child makes it to class on time. He/she is not completing their work and I have concerns that they may fall behind."

The most gut-wrenching part of the whole thing was that teachers were spending so much time chasing kids and parents who weren't responding, and yet our attendance policy was that students were "attending" if they even tried to log in to Zoom. I knew it was my responsibility to make sure that kids were learning, and I embraced that responsibility with pride, but when the kids weren't coming and I had no control over the situation, it made me doubt what the point even was in fighting for these kids. And that is the saddest and most disgusting thing I've ever felt as a teacher.

My teaching philosophy is that every single student can learn when they have the adult support needed to be successful. That means different things for every single kid. E-learning often made me feel that I was not good enough, that I did not do enough, and that I served no purpose in supporting these kids. But as I reflect on that, I am able to recognize that every single thing I said just now was wrong.

Every email, phone call, and Schoology message that I sent was my way to say that *I care about you.* I couldn't fix things for everyone, but even when things got really frustrating or felt hopeless, I didn't give up. I put in the time to make Pizza Shop fraction lessons, find a teacher or family member to join my classes as a Guest of Honor, and touch base regularly with families to share what little information I had learned about their children this year. It never felt like enough at the time because it was *nothing* compared to a pre-pandemic school year. I had no control over the world or the things happening in the homes of these families, but I had control over how I presented myself as an adult who cares about these kids and I absolutely had control over the amount of effort I put in every single day at school. I think if I don't take away anything else from this school year, I can walk away with my head held high that I gave my best fighting chance to make this year meaningful for my students. Most days, it took everything that was in me to make it happen, but I did it anyway.

March 2021
A Step in the Right Direction

ONE UNIQUE COMPONENT THAT ADDED TO THE COMPLEXITY OF THIS school year was a nationwide focus on social justice. I take pride in knowing that I do work for a district that had an emphasis and vision for how to promote social justice prior to the George Floyd protests, and this year was no exception. In fact, I feel that the nation's response to this black man being tragically killed required our staff to have conversations about race, equity, and justice at a much faster pace than what we would have had those conditions not existed.

As I write this chapter, I am very cognizant that I am an upper-middle class white American who has known privilege my whole life. I am proud to be in a multi-racial marriage, and one day I hope to have children of my own whom I can teach about racial equity. I have experienced microaggressions in my life, I have learned to stand up for others and love those who are different from me. I grew up in a small town where almost everyone was white and Catholic. I can only speak about my own experience, and I don't even want to pretend that I understand what others' experiences may be. I want to speak my truths, but I recognize that some of it may seem shallow or misguided. I may not say everything perfectly in a politically correct manner, but my intentions are pure.

I wrestled with whether or not it was okay for me to write this chapter, because it was a topic I wrestled with all year. I didn't know what my place was, and I didn't think I had the language or expertise to talk about such a sensitive topic as a white woman.

However, after reflecting on it over and over again, I do think it's okay to share about my own experience surrounding social justice because it is a process and being white doesn't mean that I can't have feelings on the matter. My hope is that by taking small steps by sharing my truths, identifying my biases, breaking down barriers, having uncomfortable conversations, mending broken relationships and owning up to my part in racial inequity that I can become a better person who people of all races can trust and respect.

In the month of February, teachers in our district were given a very specific Black History Month curriculum that had been developed over the last two years. In the midst of heightened awareness to the oppression of Black and Brown Americans, most teachers recognized the importance of teaching this content and were very aware that it would be taught in a virtual setting and that parents would have access to hear every part of it. We didn't know what type of comments or feelings the families of our students had, what was being taught in the homes. It was our responsibility to teach the students about how to treat one another and stand up for what is right, and it was our job to do that by empowering Black voices, sharing Black literature, and teaching about why the protests were happening in our city in 2020 in a language that was appropriate for their grade level. It was challenging to have some of these conversations, because at times, I felt like it was weird to be a white teacher who has never experienced social inequity in this way, who never attended a protest, or joined a social justice group could make an impact on these kids regarding this topic. I often felt like a phony, like I was trying to read a book that was written in a language that I didn't understand. I knew that I had white colleagues who were so comfortable with having these types of conversations and they sounded so well-spoken, so knowledgeable. Having been raised in a white community and teaching 95% majority white students at my previous district, I didn't feel like I was equipped to lead these conversations. I felt like I was still immature, still an infant at discussing topics like Black empowerment and understanding my own biases. I felt incompetent, like the parents and the students who listened to me teach these lessons were going to see right through me.

I often thought back to my first interview when I moved to the city. I was interviewing at a diverse school very similar to where I teach now. The principal and vice principal were both people of color and they asked me about how I would teach about cultural and racial diversity. I am now very ashamed of the answer I gave, but it was the only connection with the topic I had ever had. I told these wonderful Black men that I would teach about cultural and racial diversity when teaching lessons about the Civil War and the racial injustice that happened during slavery. Looking back now, I just drop my jaw at how stupid and incompetent I must have sounded and 100% understand why I wasn't offered that job. Now, almost five years later, I always think about how I would answer that differently and how thankful I am to have the topics of social injustice and racial or cultural equity be present almost daily in my classroom. My school challenged me to grow by forcing these types of uncomfortable conversations to happen. I know that I have such a long way to go before I can ever feel like I will be confident on this topic, but I know that every single day I have to step up and show up for my students of color. I have to teach students of every race to treat each other in a way that is kind and respectful. I have to teach my students to care for those around them and to stand up for what is right so that the next generation doesn't fall into the same patterns that those before them did. I need to have these conversations with kids because they deserve to talk about it in a way that I never did. School is no longer just about math, reading, science, and social studies. Public school is becoming a political place where students are learning about complicated adult topics, and teachers are being asked to teach about some challenging and uncomfortable things.

I watched as my students of all races began to make connections with one another in ways that I had not seen before. They felt empowered to make a difference in their world and they started to seek out videos, books, and other materials on their own that talked about famous Black Americans or social justice.

I also feel like I grew as a teacher, because I started to become painstakingly aware how "white" our curriculums are, even though we intentionally sought out diversity within our curriculums. I noticed how "white" our classrooms are. I wanted to change the way I teach because I stopped feeling like my in-person and virtual classroom space reflected the students I was teaching. I started to use more and more images of diverse peoples, even if it took a lot longer to search them on Google. I displayed texts that were intentional about including diverse characters or were written by diverse authors. There were many ways I felt like I fell through as a teacher this year, but this was one way I felt like I could make a very tiny change in myself to become better for my students and for students in years to come.

The way my students responded to the Black History Month content gave me a new passion for being a part of the change in my school building. There had been many conversations around equity and the vision that they had for creating curriculum that reflects the diverse nature of our school district. March is designated as Women's History Month in the U.S., and I wanted to create something that would engage students to bring attention to the challenges that women have overcome throughout history and show appreciation towards the women that have helped shape us into the people we are today.

I spent one full weekend meticulously planning out three weeks worth of content recognizing important female activists, women in government, and women in our community. I also wanted to put a global perspective on these topics since so many of our students and their families have immigrated to the U.S. I felt fascinated by the work

I was doing and was so excited to share it with my team members and share it with my students.

As I began implementing the Women's History Month curriculum during my closing meetings each day in March, I had students tell me how proud they are to be women and how they hope to make a difference in the world just like the women we were studying. To me, this was the most powerful and rewarding feeling. My students were feeling empowered to become amazing people that could change the world, and a big part of it was because their school and their teacher valued taking time to have some hard conversations about race and equity.

At the end of March, we had a professional development centered around Cultural Diversity and I had another lightbulb moment. Our largest school populations are comprised of Asian Americans. These students were learning so much about the Black America and equity for people of all races, but our Asian students rarely got to see themselves or their family members reflected in the lessons we were teaching. They rarely saw Asian literature, Asian culture, or even famous Asians or Asian Americans mentioned at school. My future children will be Asian, and it was deeply sad for me to realize that they may never get this kind of exposure in their education either.

I wanted my Asian students to feel pride in who they are, where they come from, and to know that they are seen too.

I had started to put some resources together, hoping that they might be completed before the month of May, which is Asian American and Pacific Islander Heritage Month. I knew that this was a huge project, and with full in-person learning coming quickly in April, I knew that it was going to take a lot of time and energy to make it happen. I decided to reach out to my colleagues to see if there was a small and mighty team of people who could help me tackle the job. The five of us worked together to produce a strong list of resources, and I am so grateful for the hard work and dedication this group of teachers put in to make it happen.

Even though there were so many areas of learning that I feel were lost this school year, I can walk away knowing that even though kids will always remember this year as the pandemic year that they had to do at-home school, they will also remember that this year was when they learned about some pretty life-changing things that helped them to become strong, courageous members of their school and their community.

April 2021
Opening Up

WE SPENT THE EARLY WEEKS OF APRIL PREPARING FOR OUR RETURN to in-person learning. Parents of students who had been remote all school year had large amounts of fear in sending their children back to school. Students who had been in their homes for more than a year were terrified that they would get sick upon coming back to school. In order to help some of these families make the transition, our school offered a "meet and greet" family night where parents and their children could come to the school, get a guided tour and meet some of the staff, and explore the classroom space where their child would be attending classes. I wanted to be a friendly face to these families, since I feel that I have a talent for making others feel welcome and at ease, so I decided to volunteer at this event.

Our building is 3-5 grades, so some of these third graders had never been in our building before. As I gave guided tours of the building, I always asked the students the same questions: What are you most looking forward to about coming back to school? What Specials class are you excited to do in person?

It was jaw-dropping to hear the most common responses: *I am just excited to do my work with a paper and pencil instead of the iPad. I am just excited to be in my classroom.*

If this was a normal start to the school year, these would *never* be the type of responses that you'd get from kids. They'd say *I'm excited to see my friends, I'm excited to learn, I'm excited for PE, lunch, or recess.* Instead, these kids were so desperate for a place that was designed for learning. Some of their home environments made it extremely difficult to focus or study. It was incredible and heartbreaking to hear how these kids no longer took for granted the ability to attend a school to learn. They knew how special and important it was, and they were longing to be back in that space even if it felt scary.

I knew I had an important job to do in our virtual and in-person classroom space too. I needed to help create an environment of trust and respect so that all kids could feel comfortable with the return to in-person coming so quickly. In early April, I had very little information about what our schedule, classroom, and procedures would look like. I decided to use 20 minutes of our virtual ELA block on Fridays to share what I did know with the kids and give them time to ask questions and process the big change that was coming. The students would ask all kinds of questions, and many of them remained without answers until right before our in-person start date.

I had a lot of reassurance as I started preparing the classroom space, as I had a larger number of in-person students during the hybrid model than many of my colleagues. I gave myself permission to try out some of the new procedures that I envisioned using with this smaller group, asked for the students' feedback about what they liked and disliked, and got them invested in getting the classroom ready for their peers.

One great example is that our building administrators gave us permission to put desks into groups of three for the first time all year, as long as they were at least three feet apart from seat to seat. I have used the "pod" structure for many years, and I felt like it would be so perfect in providing kids with a way to work in partners, teams, and even have some opportunities to socialize at a safe distance. Unfortunately, with the spacing requirement, I was unable to put the desks so that they were touching and had to find an alternative solution. I had some old baskets that I wasn't using because I had downsized my classroom library to be Covid-manageable, and I decided to tape those baskets between the desks. We used this model for about a week, and I quickly realized that the baskets were super ugly (in my opinion) and didn't have a good aesthetic look. I decided to laminate some colored table tents that had positive messages on them, like "You've got this!" or "You are valuable!" so that no matter where you were in the classroom, you were surrounded by these positive messages. When I asked kids for feedback about what they liked or disliked about the pods, they shared that they wanted to add some of their own decorations to the table tents so it felt more like their special creation rather than mine. The kids also said that they wanted to have three positive messages at each table rather than two so that everyone had their own special message. They got excited to see what each of the remote students would have on their desk and where those students would sit. They also knew that they would get to be role models and help teach the other kids how our classroom "works." It was really special and rewarding to see them start to take ownership over the classroom and turn it from my teacher-led space into our class-led space.

On April 19, we started our very first day of full day in-person learning. Every teacher was excited and nervous for how this day would go, and honestly, it was a day that we really didn't think would come during this school year. We knew that all students were going to be absolutely exhausted since they had not attended a full day of school in almost a year and a half. I tried my best to make the classroom feel welcoming by adding bright yellow streamers, smiley face balloons, posters, and upbeat music as we invited students into the room for the first time. The halls were filled with nervous and excited smiles, and my remote students were psyched to be able to see me and their classmates for the first time. Students who originally felt extremely nervous to come seemed to settle in very quickly as they learned where things were located and how different processes work in and out of the classroom.

It was kind of a bizarre feeling as we went through our first week of in-person school. It truly felt like we were in the first week of the school year, but also felt like we had given students the expectations for the end of the new year. I listened as many of my colleagues shared similar frustrations and realizations about student behavior and in our classrooms. Each time we felt ourselves get worked up because a student, whether they had been hybrid or remote, started to talk too much or said something disrespectful or didn't follow a direction that was given, we had to stop and remind ourselves that these kids truly needed to have each expectation re-modeled so they knew how to do things correctly. We needed to approach each situation with a blank slate and help kids learn how to do what we would normally expect them to do throughout the school year.

Another challenge was that the kids really did tire out quickly. Keep in mind, earlier this year they were only watching 3-5 minute mini-lessons (if they even did that independently) and now they were expected to participate in a 30 minute lesson that required strenuous thinking. They were asked to produce work that wasn't just a one sentence typing post on Schoology, and it was actually quite difficult for many of them.

The teachers in my pod would joke about how hungry these kids seemed to be all the time, and how they never knew what an appropriate time for a snack was. We would literally walk back from the lunchroom and have 3-5 kids ask us immediately if they could eat a snack. Of course, our answer was always, "Are you really hungry?" and oftentimes the kids had to stop and think twice about whether they were. The truth is, many of them probably ate whatever they wanted, whenever they wanted when they were at home.

I think one thing that was even more surprising to me was that there were a lot of kids who didn't really know how to play together. They obviously had the new added challenge of socially distancing at recess, but in general, kids had a hard time joining others or asking kids to play. They would get upset at the smallest things and have a big reaction when something didn't go the way they wanted. I volunteered to help with recess duty, and on day one I literally had two kids in a chokehold and another who was throwing people to the ground while playing tag. This isn't necessarily something I'd never seen before, but it was just shocking that these incidents were happening because "someone pushed me in tag and I didn't like it." I watched other kids hide behind playground equipment or isolate themselves and cry on the buddy bench because they didn't know what to play or who to play with. The recess supervisors decided to bring a few ideas to the PE teacher and principal so that they could support these kids in making safe, kind choices at recess and learn how to play together. The PE teachers taught the kids how to use the playground equipment appropriately and play games like tag in a safe way.

Late in the first week of in-person learning, I had an unexpected twist occur. I received a phone call on Wednesday night that I had a family member in the hospital. It was a complicated family situation, and we were all in an extreme state of grief over the circumstances. My family lives about 10 hours away from where my husband and I live, and every day I felt like I lived 1,000,000 miles away. My patience wore thin and I was emotionally exhausted from the roller coaster of information that was shared with me each night on the telephone. I knew that I had to be responsible and stay at school for that week, but it was killing me to be away from my family when I felt like they were in need. Every day when I got home from work, I would literally sit on the couch with my mouth hanging open. All I could feel or hear was silence; stillness. I felt like everything inside me was used up and that all I had left over was a shell of a person. It made me feel like a worthless wife and daughter; like I couldn't function in a way that made any sense.

Finally, on Saturday, I had reached my breaking point. Eric came running upstairs to find me in the fetal position, sobbing on the floor of our bedroom. I had just missed a call from my family member, and I had no idea if that would have been our final conversation ever. I didn't know if I'd get to see her again, and I was in absolute grief. Eric hugged me for what felt like hours, and he finally said, "Emily, I think you need to go. I'm giving you permission to take time off of work to be with your family. You don't have to if you don't think you need it, but I think you need to be there together." I continued sobbing and felt such great feelings of conflict.

Taking time off as a teacher isn't like you just call in sick in the morning and there are no concerns. It's always a huge effort pulling together last minute sub plans, making sure they know all your procedures (including Covid procedures this year), and spending a day worried that your kids are going to be extremely naughty, get into fights, and cause you to get a reputation as a terrible teacher.

I knew that if I took this time off that I was going to need a full week to do what I needed with my family. At the time, it felt like an impossible decision, but hindsight being 20/20, it was the best decision I've made in my life. I spent nearly three hours that afternoon writing out my sub plans, putting together a slideshow with all the books, visuals, and movies that I needed since I wouldn't be able to go into my classroom and prepare them. I reached out to a coworker who I trusted and asked her to print them all off for me and help the sub to get set up on Monday. We left around 7:00 that night, and made our way to my parents' house by Sunday.

This was not a restful or peaceful car ride. Rather, my anxiety was in full force; I was worried about my classroom, worried about my parents, worried about my family member, worried about my own mental health. I was worried about being worried, which felt incredibly stupid in itself. I wrestled myself to stay awake, drifting in and out of nightmares about my two worlds that felt thousands of miles apart.

I spent the next week taking care of and spending time with my grieving family. I bought groceries and managed meals when others couldn't. On two occasions, we drove two hours to make a hospital visit. Other days were spent preparing the house for our family member's return, and all in all, it was absolutely an exhausting week. I don't think I went a day without crying, and I often walked around with a dull pain in my chest from my anxiety. I spent every day worrying if things would be okay, and I had no control over my emotions.

In therapy, I learned a tool that I like to call the "5 finger tool" where you bring yourself back to the present by using your senses. I practiced using this tool over and over again in order to manage my anxiety.

What does all of this have to do with teaching? It was absolutely amazing to see how my team rose up and supported me in my time of need. I didn't tell a single person why I was out of the building, and there were only two who knew I would be out for an extended time. Every single day, I had a different team member reach out via text or phone call saying, "I noticed that you were out again today. I hope that you're doing okay; I'm here for you if you need anything." One even reminded me that there were a bunch of things like preparing our desk spaces and covering posters for IAR testing the next week, and she stepped in and just took care of it for me. Another spent her afternoon completing my testing documentation that I was unable to complete remotely. My principal and vice principal both reached out personally and asked if there was anything I needed from them.

There had been times this year where I had previously wondered if anyone would even care if I was gone, and the answer was *absolutely yes*. I had been living in my fishbowl classroom and I had forgotten what it really means to be a team. These people had nothing to gain by reaching out to me, and yet they went above and beyond to make me know that I was loved and appreciated. It was heartwarming and astounding, and it felt like such a gift to have them cover everything I needed at school so that I could be present with my family in their time of need.

I had also sent an email to my students' families on Sunday letting them know that I would be out for the week. I let them know that I was feeling safe and healthy, since we are in the era of Covid, and that I needed time away for a family emergency. I had four different families reach out and send well wishes or prayers on my behalf. I have always valued the relationships we built with parents, but let me tell you, that was one of the most powerful things I've had parents do for me. It meant so much more to me than any Starbucks gift card ever will. I think this is one precious thing about the Covid season - it taught me the importance of being real with the families we serve. When we trust each other, we can have challenging conversations, but we can also support one another in a time of need.

May 2021
The Final Chapter

BY THE TIME WE REACHED MAY, YOU STARTED TO SEE TEACHERS SINK into old habits of counting down the days (and maybe even the minutes) until the end of the school year. I think this year more than ever, there was actually a desperate longing to reach the end of the school year.

For me, when people would ask me how many days we had left of school, I often found myself unable to answer. I would like to think it's because I'm a super teacher and could do school year round, but that's not the truth at all. This school year, and especially at the time of my family crisis in early April, I was no longer able to think beyond the end of the week. I had given myself small checkpoints to make it to so that I didn't go absolutely mad.

I shared this with my therapist when she asked me that question, and she helped me to come to a really interesting conclusion. I had assumed that when the end of the school year came, I'd be beyond ready to ride off into the sunset. At one point this year, I had thought about leaving teaching already. But the reality was that even though the months of April and May felt insanely challenging and every day felt like a marathon, it was the first time all school year that I actually felt like a teacher. I actually got to teach all my subject areas, help kids figure out how to make friends, teach them what good sportsmanship is, give air hugs and high-fives, and have kids draw pictures of me as a superhero. These are the things that make teaching so precious, and these are the things that keep me coming back year after year.

The other insightful thing that my therapist asked was, "If I had asked Emily from January of 2020 what she'd think if I told her that she was going to be confined to her home and scared to death of an invisible virus during a world-wide pandemic, teach from her laptop for nearly seven months, live in a city where there was looting and protesting happening over social justice issues, experience one of the most debated presidential elections in U.S. history, have two family crises, go through the loss of a family member due to that invisible virus, and restart the structure of her school year five times over the course of 14 months?" I told her that January 2020 Emily would have laughed and said we were absolutely crazy. And sadly, the things in this memoir don't even begin to scratch the surface of the difficulties that extend into my personal life beyond teaching during a pandemic.

It is absolutely shocking to me to this day that we as a world have endured this incredible amount of stress, pain, hurt, anger, discouragement, frustration, isolation, and true loneliness during the pandemic. We have come out ahead and I hope that you feel that you've learned something about yourself through the process.

For me, I resonate on the fact that I am resilient. This pandemic wore me down, made me question everything about what it means to be happy, but it did not shut me down. I am stronger than a virus, and I will keep on fighting for what I love. I am a teacher, and 2020 has made me so painstakingly aware of the brokenness of our educational system but also so aware of what teaching is really all about.

If I can be there for my students when they are hurting, help them to gain new perspectives, and build a strong classroom community both in a classroom and on a Zoom call, then I have to know that I am doing everything I can to be the best teacher I can be. I am not perfect by a long shot, but I strive to continue growing and challenging myself to become better.

I also carry a new burden for the educational administrators of our country. While this year was extremely challenging for me, I can't imagine the burden of knowing that every single decision made surrounding Covid-19 would be questioned and that people would hate them because of it. I think the pandemic exposed flaws in our administrative systems because it required a truly unprecedented type of decision making. Never before in our history have we needed to monitor safety in a way that we did during the pandemic, and never have we been put in a potentially life-or-death situation by coming to work or by sending our children to school. I imagine these administrators have experienced their own kinds of trauma from this year, and I think we need to make it known to them how important they are and how much they are appreciated. Even if every decision they made wasn't perfect, they were asked to do an absolutely impossible task and they came out ahead. Thank you to all the administrators within my district and to those in schools around the country.

This school year will always be a year that we never forget due to the pandemic, e-learning, hybrid-learning, and in-person school. For me, there is one more reason I will never forget this year...

On May 14, I awoke to a text message from my principal telling me to call him when I was available. This is *never* a good sign, so I called him back to see what the damage was. He told me that my classroom had flooded and I would have to be displaced in the meantime. So I arrived at school early to find all of my desks and classroom materials in a different classroom, and I spent the morning trying to locate and organize everything so that there wouldn't be chaos as we entered this Friday adventure.

The school day came and went, and as expected, it was a bit on the frantic side. When I got home, my husband had also had a pretty frustrating day and was feeling at his wits end. On top of all this, we had decided to start trying to have a baby in January and I was late.

We decided to get a pregnancy test and tried not to get our hopes up that it would come back positive. We waited for the longest three minutes of our lives, but then, something happened that we never expected. There was a little plus sign and we realized that we were going from a family of two to a family of three. We were absolutely in shock, and it took us a while to get our feet under us. All the frustration and the stress of our day was suddenly wiped away and we got to celebrate the one really beautiful thing that came out of this pandemic year. There was a new peace in my heart knowing that this baby was something incredible that would mark the end of an ugly era, and that the joy in having our first baby would overshadow the pain and suffering that happened during the rest of the school year.

The final weeks of school felt like business as usual. The hustle and bustle of cleaning and disassembling a classroom while attempting to manage the behavior of students who had "signed off" and were ready for summer break finally felt like something familiar. I was permanently displaced from my classroom due to the flooding incident, so the bulk of my time was really just spent making the last few days meaningful for my kids.

What I found so sweet and sad at the end of this school year is that I had student after student come up to me and ask the same question: "Are you excited for summer or are you sad?" I would tell them that I was feeling both excited and a little sad, and they would smile and say, "Me too. I thought I was the only one who felt like that." These kids had longed for in-person school all year and I think that the speed at which it came and went felt a bit overwhelming. Even though I felt exhausted, I found myself being disappointed that the "normal" school year was ending so quickly too. I knew that the last day of school was going to be hard for a lot of kids, so I decided to make it very special for them.

I decorated the classroom with a luau theme. The walls were covered with tiki torches, flowers, and pineapples, the tables all had grass skirts, and students were greeted in the morning by choosing their favorite color of lei to wear and take home with them at the end of the day.

I chose this theme for a couple of reasons: one being that I had the decorations already from another party, but the second being that in Hawaii the word *aloha* is used to say hello and goodbye. During our morning meeting, we made a big circle like we always do, and rather than greeting each other just by saying an English *hello*, we greeted each other with a Hawaiian *aloha*. Throughout the day, kids enjoyed games, activities, and a movie to make their last day special. And finally, when it was time to leave and pack up, we made our last closing circle of the school year. Just as we had done at the start of the day, we finished with a Hawaii *aloha*, this time signaling our *good-bye and see you soon*. It felt really special, and that it was the perfect way to end a great day together.

And just like that, our school year was finished. It felt like we had been running a marathon and now we had finally reached the finish line. People were smiling again, buzzing around, ready to spend some well deserved time with their family and friends.

It felt almost like things were resuming to normal at the end of the school year because the CDC had released new mask guidelines earlier that week and Illinois was changing their policies rapidly. Masks and social distancing were no longer required for fully vaccinated people, and we were able to go out to celebrate the end of the school year with our close friends at a restaurant, indoors, for the first time.

The pandemic is not over, but there is a sense of normalcy that has begun sweeping our country for the first time in over a year. I have decided after much deliberation to continue teaching because it is what I was made to do and no pandemic is going to take that away from me. I am excited to announce our pregnancy in the coming weeks, and I can't wait to see what the year 2022 holds for our family.

I also recognize how important this book was as a part of my journey this year. I am so incredibly proud of myself for overcoming so many challenges, for staying true to the person that I was made to be, and for seeking the help that was needed when I was in crisis. Being a teacher is a hard gig, but it was excruciating to be a teacher during the pandemic. I feel a sense of resiliency as I move forward, knowing that I was able to endure 2020-2021 and all of its obstacles: an invisible virus, a stay-at-home order that lasted months, Zoom school, social justice protesting in my city and neighborhood, anxiety attacks, social isolation, death of a family member due to Covid-19, family crisis, hybrid learning, and full-time in-person learning.

And what's more is that I know I am not alone in this. Thousands of people experienced these same difficulties in different capacities, and I hope that by listening to my story that there is some sense of hope, determination, or even just peace in knowing that we are not alone. Covid-19 did its best to shake us down, tear us apart, and isolate us, but we are greater than this invisible virus.

We are *invincible*, and we will come out on the other side stronger than we ever were before.

CPSIA information can be obtained
at www.ICGtesting.com
Printed in the USA
JSRC031650040622
26161JS00001BD/28